D1175853

Local Murder
(The Maroon Cortina)

A Thriller

Peter Whalley

Samuel French – London
New York – Sydney – Toronto – Hollywood

REF
PR
6073
.H35
L8   1987

4.   Rights of Performance by Amateurs are controlled by SAMUEL FRENCH LTD, 52 FITZROY STREET, LONDON W1P 6JR, and they, or their authorized agents, issue licences to amateurs to give performances of this play on payment of a fee. **It is an infringement of the Copyright to give any performance or public reading of the play before the fee has been paid and the licence issued.**

5.   Licences are issued subject to the understanding that it shall be made clear in all advertising matter that the audience will witness an amateur performance; that the names of the authors of the plays shall be included on all announcements and on all programmes; and that the integrity of the author's work will be preserved.

The Royalty Fee indicated below is subject to contract and subject to variation at the sole discretion of Samuel French Ltd.

> Basic fee for each and every
> performance by amateurs   Code M
> in the British Isles

In Theatres or Halls seating Six Hundred or more the fee will be subject to negotiation.

In Territories Overseas the fee quoted above may not apply. A fee will be quoted on application to our local authorized agent, or if there is no such agent, on application to Samuel French Ltd, London.

6.   The Professional Rights in this play are controlled by HARVEY UNNA AND STEPHEN DURBRIDGE, 24 Pottery Lane, London W11 4LZ.

The publication of this play does not imply that it is necessarily available for performance by amateurs or professionals, either in the British Isles or Overseas. Amateurs and professionals considering a production are strongly advised in their own interests to apply to the appropriate agents for consent before starting rehearsals or booking a theatre or hall.

ISBN 0 573 01655 0

72590380

LOCAL MURDER

First presented at the Liverpool Playhouse Studio on 30th May, 1984, under the title *The Maroon Cortina*, with the following cast of characters:

Barry Clark	Ron Donachie
Janice Clark, his wife	Lynda Rooke
Alan Clark, their son	Joe Searby
Ron Pine	John North
Pauline Pine, his wife	Annie Tyson
Detective-Constable Curtiss	David Ericsson

Directed by Richard Brandon
Designed by Phil Cutts

The action of the play takes place in the through lounge of a modern semi-detached house in the north of England

ACT I   SCENE 1   An afternoon in winter
        SCENE 2   Later that evening

ACT II   SCENE 1   Three days later. Morning
        SCENE 2   The afternoon of the same day
        SCENE 3   That evening

Time—the present

ACT I*

The set is the through lounge of a modern, semi-detached house in the north of England. An afternoon in winter

There are two doors: one to the kitchen and back door; the other to the hallway, front door and staircase. There is a window at one end. Carpets and wallpaper are strongly patterned. Furniture is G-Plan. There is a small bar with pub-type optics, a picture of the Sacred Heart and a crucifix, a stacked stereo-unit, some framed family photographs and clusters of cheap ornaments. There are no books. A couple of birthday cards stand on display on a sideboard

Janice Clark and Ron Pine are sitting together. Both have cups of coffee and are smoking cigarettes

Janice Clark is in her late thirties, the lady of the house. She is attractive and normally high-spirited but has been put on edge by recent events so that her reactions at the moment are erratic and unpredictable. Her visitor, Ron Pine, is about her age, a sales engineer. He wears a suit, shirt and tie, though the neck of the shirt is undone, the tie askew and the suit wearing shiny

A silence. Ron stubs out his cigarette, gazes round the room. Then:

Ron Life has to go on though.
Janice It will. I'm just not in mood for sex, that's all.
Ron (*in protest*) Oh . . .
Janice Anyway, state my nerves are in, I don't think I could lie still long enough.
Ron I came to see how you were. (*Then he adds*) And anyway there's your Alan in th'house, in't there.
Janice Yeah.
Ron How is he? Is he, er . . . all right is he?
Janice Why ask me?
Ron You're his mother.
Janice So? He tells me nowt. He practically lives up in that room. We never seen him down here.
Ron What does he do all time?
Janice (*shrugging*) Got a telly. And a dart-board. Though what he's probably doing now . . .

---

*N.B. Paragraph 3 on page ii of this Acting Edition regarding photocopying and video-recording should be carefully read.

Ron Yeah?

Janice He's probably wondering what the hell you're doing down here.

Ron Me?

Janice Yeah. Middle of th'afternoon ...

Ron Well, er, old friend of the family, aren't I.

Janice Oh, that's what you are, is it.

Ron Well, all right, if you want summat specific ...

Janice Not me, love, no. But our Alan might.

Ron Say I've called wi' a birthday present for you.

Janice And what when he says let's have a look?

Ron Tell him he can't. It's a diamond-studded G-string and you're wearing it.

Janice (*wincing*) You've an uncomfortable imagination, you have. (*She shakes her head*) I don't know why you've come today, Ron. I don't honestly.

Ron I wanted to see how you were!

Janice I'm frigid.

Ron Not that.

Janice And I'll be round the twist as well if this goes on for much longer.

Ron Have you had much, you know, newspaper reporters, that sort of thing?

Janice (*shaking her head*) They've been sniffing round neighbours but ... haven't been here.

Ron Oh.

Janice I mean what could they say? Tell us, Mrs Clark, has it affected your life in any way having your son suspected of murder ... ?

Ron No.

Janice Mind you, we've had some letters.

Ron Letters ... ?

Janice Anonymous.

Ron Oh.

Janice One wi' no stamp on. Course me—thick as they come—I pay excess postage on it, don't I!

Ron is amused

They're not funny when you read 'em.

Ron (*ceasing being amused*) No, I'm sure, er ...

Janice Stuff they say. We know he did it. Going to be his turn next.

Ron Some sick minds aren't there ... !

Janice I got a card that was nice. (*She goes to find it*)

Ron A card ... ?

Janice I thought it was for me birthday but it's all sort of religious. Well, that way inclined. (*She reads*) "Thinking of you in your time of trouble." (*She opens it*) "Come up to me, all ye that labour and are heavy laden, and I will give you rest."

Ron Who sent it?

Janice Saint Matthew. (*Then*) Oh! (*She laughs*) Oh, sent? I thought you said said! (*She laughs*)

Ron No.

Janice Sent . . . ! Oh, er Mr and Mrs Wilson. That old couple next-door but one.

Ron Very nice.

Janice Makes a change from all th'obscenities.

Ron (*looking at his watch*) I shall have to go in ten minutes.

Janice You know what I find really peculiar though.

Ron What?

Janice When folk say that they're sure that he's innocent. I mean them that have rung up, relatives and them. They're sure that he's innocent.

Ron What's peculiar about that?

Janice I'm not.

Ron You're . . . ?

Janice I'm not sure!

Ron (*in protest*) Oh . . .

Janice I don't know whether he killed her or not! *I* don't know and I'm his mother! And they all go on. (*She mimics*) "Oh, we know it'll come out all right in th'end . . . we know they'll find it's somebody else" . . . I mean they're just as stupid as them anonymous letters that say they know he did it!

Ron (*calming her*) Hey, hey . . . (*And he takes her in his arms*)

Janice I don't bloody know and I'm his bloody mother!

Ron Come on, come on . . .

And they stand silent, arms round one another for a moment

Janice Do you think he's innocent?

Ron Course I do.

Janice There's no course about it! (*She breaks away from him*) For God's sake, Ron, that's what I'm saying!

Ron All right . . .

Janice There's no course about it!

Ron (*taking her in his arms again*) All right . . .

Janice I'm not saying I think he's guilty.

Ron I know.

Janice Just that . . .

Ron You don't know.

Janice I don't. And I don't know how anybody else can say they do either.

Ron Yeah.

Janice Must sound awful. Coming from me.

Ron No.

A pause. She rests her head on his shoulder, growing calm. He glances at the hall door

He's, er, he's not liable to come down, your Alan, is he?

Janice No.

Ron Oh.

Janice If he does we'll do what you said, tell him you're giving me me birthday present. A quick screw.

Ron (*encouraged*) Funny you should mention that . . .
Janice (*breaking away from him*) Get lost!

Ron gives a little laugh to show that it was a joke. Janice lights another cigarette

Ron Going to have to go. I'm supposed to be in Blackburn selling hydraulic rams.

Janice gives him a look

   I am.
Janice If you say so.
Ron Hey and look, are you sure that you want us to come tonight?
Janice Yeah.
Ron No, I just thought . . .
Janice If I have to spend another night by meself listening to Barry chunnering on about how police are trying to frame our Alan and how he's not going to let 'em get away wi' it, I'll . . . (*She shakes her head*) Oh yeah, you've got to come!
Ron Yeah, right, fine. He did seem a bit, er, uptight over the phone did Barry.
Janice Uptight . . . !
Ron Well . . .
Janice If he gets any further up or any tighter they'll be taking him away in a green van.
Ron Not surprising though is it.
Janice He knows our Alan's innocent.
Ron Well, I'll depart wi' me vows of chastity unbroken for once then.
Janice Make you appreciate me more next time.
Ron I always appreciate you.
Janice Yeah.
Ron Every time.
Janice (*suddenly tearful*) Oh Ron . . .

They embrace

Ron All right. I'm here.
Janice I know. And I'm glad. I don't know what I'd do wi'out you, I don't, honest.

The doorbell rings. They look at one another in surprise and quickly step apart

Ron Who . . . ?
Janice Dunno. 'Less it's for our Alan. (*As she moves to answer it*) And what are we saying? You've called to give me me birthday present . . . ?
Ron Yeah.
Janice So what is it?
Ron It's a surprise.

Janice gives up. She goes off to answer the front door

Ron waits and listens. The front door is opened

Janice (*off*) Oh.
Curtiss (*off*) Hello, Mrs Clark.
Janice (*off*) You want to come in?
Curtiss (*off*) Yes please.

Ron adopts the pose of a casual visitor to the house. Curtiss' voice is not one that he recognizes

   The front door is closed. Janice leads Curtiss into the room

Detective-Constable Curtiss is in the local CID. Aged thirty. Casually dressed. Mild-mannered

Janice Police.
Ron Ah.
Curtiss Afternoon.
Ron How do.
Janice We'll see you tonight then.
Ron Yeah.
Janice Give Pauline my love.
Ron I will. And I'll tell her you liked your present.
Janice Yes.
Ron (*enjoying the joke*) She was worried about the size.
Janice (*who isn't*) Was she.
Ron Bye then. (*And a nod to Curtiss*)
Curtiss Cheers.

   Ron goes out

   Your birthday then, is it.
Janice Yeah. So what d'you want?
Curtiss A word wi' Alan if he's about.
Janice He's not, no. He's not in.
Curtiss (*surprised*) He's not?
Janice No.
Curtiss His bike's outside.
Janice Why don't you talk to that then? Or do you not talk Japanese?

Curtiss smiles patiently

   What is it you want him for anyway?
Curtiss Oh, just clear up one or two details, you know. He hasn't left the
   area, anything like that, has he?
Janice No.
Curtiss Right then. (*He moves to leave*) I daresay he'll turn up sooner or
   later . . .

Janice, seeing him out, opens the hall door. She gives a cry of surprise on finding:

   *Alan standing there, blocking the doorway. Alan Clark is aged eighteen.
   Short hair. Wears T-shirt, jeans, trainers. Well-built. Shy, reserved, even
   sullen*

Well.

Janice For God's sake ... !

Alan comes past Janice, into the room

What do you want to go doing a trick like that for?

Alan You that's doing tricks.

Janice And don't give me your clever answers!

Curtiss All right, Alan?

Alan Yeah.

Janice Just come in, have you?

Alan Just come into this room, yeah.

Janice Well, he wants to talk to you. Only you're not to say a word. Not till I've told your dad what's going on.

Alan What do you have to tell him for?

Janice Well, he'll go balmy if I don't, won't he!

Alan They'll only take me in again!

Janice They can't.

Alan Course they can.

Curtiss smiles, saying nothing. Janice hesitates, undecided. Then:

Janice I'm going to ring your dad. (*To Curtiss*) You can't stop me doing that! You can't stop me using me own phone!

Curtiss Last thing in the world, love. I'd have British Telecom on me back if I did.

Janice (*to Alan*) I'm sure I should get that solicitor, that Mr Grady.

Alan Go and ring me dad if it'll make you any happier.

Janice goes

Curtiss closes the door after her

Curtiss Good lad.

Alan I want to go out tonight, that's all.

Curtiss Oh ay? Where?

Alan Speedway.

Curtiss You're not working?

Alan shakes his head

Rest and recuperation is it?

Alan shrugs

There's only one way you'll ever get any right rest, you know that, don't you.

Alan What?

Curtiss Get if off your chest. Tell me all about it.

Alan (*sighing; he's been through this a dozen times*) Nowt to tell.

Curtiss How have you been sleeping?

Alan In me bed.

Curtiss (*not amused*) I'm sticking me neck out here you know. Should be taking you down station be rights. (*Then*) You know what your mother said just now? When I asked her if you were in?

Alan Said I weren't.

Curtiss Yeah. Now I think that's a natural reaction is that. Somebody puts something to you, first thing you do is deny it. Did you do that? No! It were him, it were anybody, it weren't me! Natural reaction. But then when you've had time to think about it, time to reflect . . .

Alan I've told you. It weren't me.

Curtiss Alan, it's not going to end. It's not going to go away. It's going to be one long nightmare . . . on and on . . . till you tell somebody and get shut of it.

Janice comes in from the hall

Janice He's coming. I've rung your dad and he's coming straight home now.

Alan shrugs: So what?

Curtiss We shan't be long anyway, shall we, Alan?

Janice And you don't have to answer. Your dad says you don't have to answer owt!

Alan I know.

Janice (*to Curtiss*) Haven't you asked him everything there is to ask? You had him at that police-station for two days!

Curtiss I know. I was there with him. My wife wasn't too pleased.

Janice, annoyed and unhappy about the situation, looks from one to the other. Then goes out to the kitchen. Slams the door

So, Alan.

Alan What?

Curtiss You were going to tell me.

Alan Were I.

Curtiss Look, if you want to play games then OK, we'll play 'em by the book, down the station. But you won't be out in time for your speedway, I can promise you that.

Alan If I say what you want me to say then I'll never be out in time for any speedway, will I.

Curtiss looks at him, opens his notebook

Curtiss Let's go over the details then, shall we. Tell me all over again what happened last Sat'day, eh.

Alan I got up. Had me breakfast. Cleaned me teeth . . .

Curtiss (*stopping him*) Hey, hey, what's all this clever stuff, eh?

Alan You said tell you . . .

Curtiss I know what I said. And you know what I meant. What time did your mates call for you?

Alan Half-eight.

Curtiss And they were Billy Hindle and Trevor Hutchinson, yeah?

Alan Yeah.

Curtiss Trevor were telling me he's a bit of a footballer. Had a trial wi' Man City.

Alan So?

Curtiss So ... great.

Alan Didn't get on though, did he.

Curtiss Most of us don't even manage to get to a trial, do we. (*Then he smiles*) No pun intended.

Alan No what?

Curtiss I wasn't trying to make a joke about trial.

Alan Didn't do, did you.

Curtiss So, the three of you, you go along to the *Waggoner's Arms*. Where there's a disco. But you have a drink in the bar first, yeah?

Alan Yeah.

Curtiss Who got 'em in?

Alan Billy I think.

Curtiss Why's that, 'cause he's under age?

Alan Why don't you arrest him then?

Curtiss What time did you go into the disco?

Alan Half-nine.

Curtiss And what time did you leave?

Alan Twenty-past eleven.

Curtiss With Amanda.

Alan No.

Curtiss Well, it wasn't wi' Billy or Trevor, was it.

Alan By meself.

Curtiss 'Cause they left wi', er ... (*He consults his notebook*) Susan Greenhalgh and Millicent Knight. I tell you what, she's a funny girl that Millicent, don't you think?

Alan shrugs

He'd be better off wi' Man City would Trevor, he would. How much did you have to drink?

Alan Three pints of lager.

Curtiss Plus one in the bar before you went in.

Alan Four.

Curtiss I mean you were all tanked up, weren't you. Sat'day night fever and all that. And your two mates had clicked. Even if Trevor does live to regret it. And you'd met Amanda.

No response

Who fancied you.

No response

(*Incredulous*) And you went home on your own?

Alan Yeah.

Curtiss Come on, Alan.

Alan I did.

Curtiss I mean you do like girls, don't you.

Alan Some of 'em.

Curtiss I mean you're not queer.

Alan Would it get me off if I said I were?

Curtiss No.

Alan Well, I'm not then.

Curtiss And I mean you liked Amanda. (*He goes to the window*) Amanda who's now dead. But who used to live across the road. Was that her bedroom window, that front one?

Alan How should I know?

Curtiss I thought you might have been in it.

No response

I mean that time you went out with her. Before your mother warned you off.

Alan She didn't warn me off.

Curtiss Didn't exactly encourage you, did she. She reminded you that Amanda, God rest her soul, was a little tart. Already had what's generally referred to as a reputation. Didn't she?

Alan I knew anyway.

Curtiss So you didn't take her out anymore. Your mother laid the law down and you didn't take her out anymore. And then there she was. At this disco. Did she know that you were going?

Alan No.

Curtiss Did you know that she was going?

Alan No.

Curtiss Must have been Fate then, eh?

Alan You said that before.

Curtiss Did I. Yeah well, I don't have many jokes.

Alan I'd noticed.

Curtiss Summat else I've said before then. And this is no joke. You were with that girl on Saturday night. We've got forensic evidence. We've got specimens of your hair that was on her and her make-up that was on you. And we've looked at 'em through microscopes and telescopes and everything else that you can think of.

Alan I told you.

Curtiss Tell me again.

Alan We went for a walk round.

Curtiss When?

Alan Half-ten.

Curtiss Where?

Alan Car-park.

Curtiss Why?

Alan She wanted some fresh air.

Curtiss Fresh air . . . ?

Alan Yeah.

Curtiss Round here? (*Then*) But, come on, Alan, this is supposed to be when you got her make-up over your jacket . . .

Alan I told you. She started . . .

Curtiss Started getting fruity.
Alan Yeah.
Curtiss But you remembered what mummy had told you.

No response

And you took her back into the disco. (*Then*) Hey, how did you get back in?
Alan (*surprised: this is a new question*) We had pass-outs.
Curtiss Don't give pass-outs, do they?
Alan (*hesitating, then*) They do.
Curtiss I've been back there this morning. Talking to people. (*A pause*) See, it doesn't stand up, does it.
Alan Well, what do you call 'em if they're not pass-outs ... tickets ... passes ...
Curtiss You never went back, Alan.
Alan I did!
Curtiss When you took her out of that disco that was when you took her home. Up this avenue. And down that lane at the end.
Alan (*shouting*) They give pass-outs! They're pink! So don't bloody try and con me that they don't!
Curtiss (*calming*) All right ...

But Janice comes from the kitchen

Janice Hey! And what's going on?
Alan Nowt.
Janice So what's all this shouting for? What's he been saying?
Alan Nowt.
Janice (*looking from one to the other*) You don't have to tell him owt you know.
Alan Oh, leave it, Mam ...
Janice And he'll be here in a minute anyway. Will your dad.
Alan Yeah.

Janice exits to the kitchen

A pause

They give pass-outs.
Curtiss (*nodding, then*) And was that when she told you that she was pregnant? When you went walkabout?
Alan No.
Curtiss It was afterwards then, was it? When you took her home?
Alan I never took her home. She never told me.
Curtiss Who told you then?
Alan You did.
Curtiss Who do you think was the father?
Alan Dunno.
Curtiss Might have been you.
Alan No.
Curtiss Could have been you.

Alan No.

Curtiss Well, come on, Alan, how long is it since you went out with her? Before your mother said leave her alone, she's mucky? How long?

Alan You know.

Curtiss Two months.

Alan (*sarcastic*) Yeah, and she were two months' pregnant! Well, well, well!

Curtiss (*a gesture of helplessness*) It's like a jigsaw, isn't it. It dun't seem to matter what we do. Break it up. Shuffle up the pieces. All falls back into the same picture.

Alan No.

Curtiss Does for me.

Alan Dun't for me.

Curtiss Two months ago you have your little fling with Amanda . . .

Alan (*in protest: not again*) Oh . . .

Curtiss (*persevering*) Two months ago, right? Then your parents come the heavy. They say stay away from the little slag, she's bad news. So you do. I mean for one thing, I bet your dad'd give you a hiding if you didn't, wouldn't he?

Alan He'll be here in a minute.

Curtiss Then two months later—last Sat'day night—disco—four pints of lager—you and Amanda get it together again. You walk her home.

Alan No.

Curtiss Then you get outside here and it's young love's eternal problem. Where do you go? You haven't got a motor. Seating arrangements on your bike aren't exactly conducive. So, all right, it has to be down the back lane.

Alan You told me she hadn't had sex.

Curtiss Not that night, no.

Alan Right.

Curtiss But that was because what rather spoilt the party was when she let on that she was in the club. Something that she'd discovered with the help of her local chemist only twenty-four hours earlier. And she says—it's down to you, Alan, she says. It's going to have your curly, black hair, she says. I mean perhaps she dun't actually know 'cause she's got a very crowded diary has Amanda. But she fancies you anyway. So she says— it's down to you, Alan.

Alan Crap.

Curtiss Well, that's what you say, yes. Only she gets stroppy. She starts shouting about what she's going to do, who she's going to tell. And you think of your dad and your mam . . . and you put up them big, strong hands to stop her . . .

As Alan has begun to laugh

What's funny about that? What's funny about a young girl being strangled?

Alan (*shaking his head*) I thought . . . when you came here . . .

Curtiss Yeah?

Alan I thought you must have summat new to ask me. But you haven't, have you.
Curtiss Oh, haven't I.
Alan No.

A pause. Curtiss goes to the window

Curtiss I'll tell you what's new, Alan. You want to know what's new?
Alan What?
Curtiss I've been talking to Billy and Trev again.
Alan And?
Curtiss Well, they did their best—I mean, mates aren't they—but when it came to it they couldn't give you any help at all.
Alan What d'you mean?
Curtiss They can't remember you going out of that disco with Amanda and then coming back in again. Not even for ten minutes. (*Then he notices through the window*) Cavalry's here.
Alan You what?
Curtiss Listen, Alan. I know—I mean I *know*—that you killed that girl.
Alan Then you know nowt, do you.
Curtiss It's down to you, Alan. And in my book it's going to stay down to you.

Barry Clark enters, hurrying in from the front door. He is a powerfully-built man in his late thirties

Barry Right. You. Out.
Curtiss Hello, Mr Clark.

And Janice comes from the kitchen

Janice He said he wanted to talk to him ...
Barry All right.
Janice I didn't know what to do!
Barry Well, he's done talking now.
Curtiss I think we have as a matter of fact, yeah.
Barry (*to Alan*) What's he said?
Alan Nowt fresh.
Janice I didn't know whether to let him in or what!
Barry Not easy to keep out. Same as cockroaches.
Curtiss No call to get abusive.
Barry Come on. Out. If I wanted coppers in my house I'd have stuck a bundle of fivers behind toilet.
Curtiss Think about what I've said, Alan, won't you. Bye, Mrs Clark.

He goes

No-one moves until the front door has closed

Barry What has he said?
Alan Nowt.
Barry Oh well, you can think about that all you like. (*Then*) I hope you're not keeping owt back.

Alan I'm not.

Barry 'Cause they'll pin it on you if they can you know. When it comes to hey lads hey all they're after is keeping their books straight.

Alan I know.

Janice You've said, Barry ...

Barry Well, I'm saying it again, aren't I!

Janice Yeah.

Barry Have to find somebody, won't they. A thing like this, they won't just let it drop!

Janice Are you stopping or going back to th'arcade?

Barry Stopping. There's nowt much doing anyway.

Janice I've got some coffee on. (*To Alan*) Do you want a cup?

Alan No.

Janice No, thank you!

Barry You're sure he didn't say owt different?

Alan Sure. I reckon he must fancy me. Just wanted th'excuse to see me again.

Alan goes out to the hall and upstairs

Barry (*amused*) Reckons he must fancy him ... !

Janice (*not amused*) You want a cup of coffee?

Barry No. (*And he pours himself a whisky*)

Janice Oh hey, Barry, you're not starting drinking already?

Barry Am I not.

Janice You know we've got Ron and Pauline coming tonight.

Barry Gone sundown han't it. Or whatever it's supposed to be.

Janice It's sodding November, Barry! It'd gone sundown at half-past-three!

Barry Not my fault.

Janice I don't want you kaylied before they get here.

Barry Did *you* hear owt of what that copper were saying?

Janice No.

Barry He's a clever bugger that one. He could piss round corners that one.

Janice (*tutting*) Your language, honestly! Getting as common as muck!

Barry Company I keep. (*Then*) He were one of them that tried to do me at th'arcade you know. When the Paki were found wi' them drugs on him.

Janice You said.

Barry Tried to make out as I knew what were going on. That I were letting 'em use place. I reckon that's what's behind this you know. Getting their own back on me through our Alan.

Janice Well 'appen. But they've let him go, haven't they.

Barry Makes no odds. That's what I'm trying to get through to you! What I'm trying to get through to him! All right, we know our Alan's innocent. Everybody that knows him knows he's innocent. But they'll still pin it on him if they get half a flaming chance!

Janice So what have they let him go for then?

Barry 'Cause they haven't got a case. It's all what's-it ... circumstantial.

Janice So they can't do owt.

Barry Not unless they come up wi' a witness, no.

Janice But I mean, if he's innocent ...

Barry looks at her

    I mean wi' him being innocent, then there can't be any witness, can there.
Barry Can't be a straight 'un.
Janice No.
Barry Can be bent witnesses though, can't there. Bent owt. Been bent Popes before today.
Janice I just wish they'd hurry up and catch whoever did it.

Barry gets himself another drink

    I'm only making us a light tea 'cause we'll be having some supper later. You like pizzas, don't you?
Barry (*distracted*) Yeah. (*Then*) Listen, er, summat I've been thinking.
Janice What?
Barry It's to do wi' Ron.
Janice (*taken aback*) Ron ... ? (*And a little laugh*)
Barry Ron, yeah.

And, to her consternation, Barry carefully closes the hall door before continuing

    What do you ... you know, what do you think about him?
Janice (*defensive*) Well. They're friends of ours, aren't they. Ron and Pauline.
Barry I mean he's another clever bugger in his way is Ron. If he ever met that copper they could piss round corners at one another.
Janice Why anyway? Why're you asking me?
Barry (*looking at her, then*) Do you think Ron could have killed that girl?
Janice That ...
Barry Yeah.
Janice Amanda ... ?
Barry Haven't been any more killed round here, have there. Listen. I'll try and explain, right. And then you tell me what you think.
Janice I think this business is getting on top of you.
Barry Oh, bloody great!
Janice Well ...
Barry I said listen and then tell me your stupid opinion! Not tell it me before I've had chance to open me mouth!
Janice (*sighing*) Go on.

Barry goes to get another drink

    And I wish you'd stop drinking.
Barry And I wish you'd stop talking.

A pause. She waits

    To start wi'. Ron knew her.
Janice Knew ... ?
Barry Amanda! Ron knew Amanda!

Janice Yeah, all right, I suppose he did, yeah!

Barry He put her on to that job at Nightingales. 'Cause—remember?— you'd talked to Amanda's mother who'd said that she was leaving school and looking for a job and you'd asked Ron if there was owt going at his place . . . ?

Janice Yeah. All right, I know.

Barry So. He knew her.

Janice She'd left Nightingales though, han't she? She were on dole.

Barry So?

Janice I'm just saying.

Barry Well, I'm just saying that he knew her!

Janice nods

That's number one.

Janice Number one what?

Barry Number one . . . argument!

Janice Oh.

Barry Flaming hell . . . ! (*Then*) Number two. This is number two argument, right?

Janice Yes.

A pause

Barry Hell fire, you've made me forget what I were going to say now! (*Then*) No! I know. Ron, he's a . . . well, he's a randy bastard.

Janice looks at him. She laughs

He is!

Janice That's number two argument is it?

Barry All right, you might not see it like that. He might be just good old Ron to you. Just take my word for it, though. He's had more than his fair share has Ron. Has had a few other people's share as well.

Janice Really.

Barry That's why he's so keen on that job of his. Sales engineer. Out on the road. I mean Pauline never knows where he is, does she. I tell you. One of this town's leading fornicators is Ron.

Janice You sound jealous.

Barry Course I'm bloody jealous.

Janice Anyway, how does being this town's leading fornicator make him a murderer?

Barry That girl were up the spout, weren't she?

Janice You mean pregnant.

Barry I do.

Janice I believe she were, yeah.

Barry And if that were why she were killed—if whoever killed her killed her because she were pregnant—then th'odds are it were a married man, right?

Janice (*shrugging*) There's a lot of them about.

Barry Well. I haven't finished yet.

Janice There's a number three is there.

Barry There bloody is, yeah.

Janice Go on.

Barry Well, you know what worries me, that they'll try and stick it on our Alan ...

Janice Yeah.

Barry I mean if they don't come up wi' anybody else then they're going to try and stick it on him. So I've been, er, you know, asking around a bit.

Janice About what?

Barry Oh, who this girl knew. Who she went out wi'. Who came to see her.

Janice Yeah ... ?

Barry I got talking to Dennis Piper, you know newsagent's ...

Janice (*nodding*) Hmm.

Barry Well, I were asking him if he'd noticed owt. 'Cause you know what he's like, he's a nosey old sod.

Janice And he'll say owt about anybody if it suits him.

Barry 'Appen. Anyhow, he says he's noticed a car.

Janice Yeah?

Barry Yeah.

Janice (*sarcastic*) A real car? What, on road were it ...

Barry Listen!

Janice Well ... !

Barry He says that he's noticed this car parked in this avenue regular. Been down here for past six months, he reckons ... oh, 'appen a couple of afternoons a week.

Janice (*quietly*) So?

Barry It were a maroon Cortina. Now who does that put you in mind of?

Janice I see.

Barry Yeah.

Janice And that's it, is it?

Barry As far as I've got, yeah.

Janice And you want to know what I think?

Barry nods

It's like I said. I think this business's getting on top of you.

Barry Oh great!

Janice Well!

Barry Bloody great!

Janice You go on about police trying to pin it on Alan, now you're as bad trying to pin it on Ron!

Barry I'm not trying to pin it on him, am I hell as like!

Janice Sounds like it.

Barry It adds up though, dun't it? It all adds up!

Janice And did your friend Dennis the Menace tell you that there were a maroon Cortina parked up here today?

Barry No.

Janice Well there were.

Barry Ron's?

Janice Yeah.

Barry How do you know?

Janice 'Cause he were calling here.

Barry Here?

Janice Yeah. Called to see me. On account of he wanted to check that everything were still OK for tonight.

Barry Oh. Well. Dun't explain all them other times though, does it?

Janice Well, there's nowt to explain is there. 'Cept some daft story that you've got from a cross-eyed newsagent! I mean for Christ's sake, Barry! It in't going to do our Alan any good you know, coming up wi' loony stories about Ron! And you know they're coming tonight, him and Pauline, don't you?

Barry Yeah.

Janice Only it might just, you know, spoil th'atmosphere a bit if you start accusing him of murder!

Barry does not respond

I'm going to make us some tea.

Janice goes out to the kitchen

Barry still dissatisfied, takes another drink

The Lights fade to Black-out

SCENE 2

The same. Later the same evening

The room is as earlier but with the curtains drawn and the lights on. Bowls of crisps and nuts have been put out. Barry, Janice, Ron and Pauline are sitting round and have been so for a while. Music is playing: a tape of The Drifters or similar. We will come to the end of the tape within the first two or three minutes

Pauline, the only member of the group whom we have not already met, is Ron's wife. In her mid-thirties. Rather a neat and tidy lady, attractive but sexless

Pauline Well, by that time, I'd had it up to here. I mean it'd just been one of those days. One of those had-it-up-to-here days.

Ron It's them never-had-it-at-all days I don't like, eh Barry?

Barry, mid-way between drunk and sober, looks at him but does not respond

Pauline So, anyway, she comes in. She says I'd like to make a complaint. I said yes madam. I mean I was very civil.

Ron You didn't just tell her to sod off.

Pauline No.

Ron Anyway, you haven't told 'em best part. What had happened earlier.

Pauline Oh, you mean the . . .

Ron Him at dinnertime!

Pauline (*tutting, then reluctantly*) There was this young man at lunchtime. I'd only just eaten. And he was sick—and I don't just mean not well—I mean vomited . . .

Janice Oh dear.

Pauline All over our house-plant display.

Ron They tell folk they can bring things back! That's what he were doing!

Pauline (*patiently*) Yes, dear.

Ron Within his rights!

Janice That reminds me. I've got them pizzas to put on. Else we'll be here all night. Nobody object to pizzas, do they?

Ron No. Lovely.

Pauline gives him a little sideways glance of surprise. Then gives a little laugh of disbelief

What?

Pauline Nothing.

Janice Does he not like pizzas?

Ron Yeah!

Pauline If he says he does . . .

Ron I do!

Another little laugh of disbelief from Pauline

Janice *You* like 'em, Pauline?

Pauline Oh yes. Anything foreign.

Janice Right, well, I'll put 'em on then.

But, before she can go:

Barry Hey.

Janice What?

Barry I don't want any.

Janice You . . . !

Barry You know I can't stomach that Eyetie muck.

Janice I don't know any such thing! I told you what I was going to do. Why didn't you open your big mouth and say summat?

Barry Saying now, aren't I.

Pauline (*in sympathy*) He's (*Ron*) as bad.

Janice Well listen, we're having pizzas, right? If you want summat else then you can have summat else but we're having pizzas, right?

Barry All I'd like to know.

Janice What?

Barry How many Eyeties do you think there are sitting down tonight to fish, chips and mushy peas?

Janice sighs, gives up and exits to the kitchen

Ron (*amused*) Not so bloody many I'll bet! Or Indians or Chinese either! We have chicken chow mein and flied lice till it comes out of us lug-holes but do they have Lancashire hot-pot in Shanghai . . . ?

Pauline Yes, all right . . .
Ron Do they buggery!
Pauline I think we all take the point.
Ron Nice one, Barry lad. I like it.
Barry (*ignoring that*) Am I th'only one supping in this place . . . (*And he goes to get himself another drink*)
Ron I'll have another beer. If there's one going.

Which Barry will provide. But gracelessly, placing it so that Ron has to move to collect it

Pauline I'm all right, thank you. (*She moves to the kitchen door, from where she can converse with the unseen Janice*) So, anyway, this woman said I'd like to make a complaint. I said yes madam.
Janice (*off*) Yeah?
Pauline She said I bought these slacks yesterday. Supposed to be waist twenty-six and when I got 'em home I couldn't get into 'em.
Janice (*off*) Oh.
Ron Cheers. (*For the beer*)
Pauline And I looked at her. And honestly, if she were twenty-six well I'm . . . (*To Ron*) What's her on television?
Ron Angela Rippon.
Pauline Lorraine Chase. If she were twenty-six well then I'm Lorraine Chase. So I said, would madam like me to measure her? Well, that did it. Are you calling me fat? she said. Are you saying that I'm fat? And like I said, I'd already had it up to here what with one thing and another . . .
Ron Folk bringing their food back . . .
Pauline I said madam, all I'm saying is that our slacks know what size they are. I just wonder whether you know what size you are.

Janice enters from the kitchen

Janice Yeah?
Pauline Course that did it!
Janice I'll bet. (*To Barry*) Do I not get a drink then?
Barry You know where they are.
Janice Oh charming. (*She gets herself a drink*)
Pauline She was going to write to our Head Office. Write to her MP. I don't know who she wasn't going to write to.
Ron You getting any shooting done nowadays, Barry?
Barry No.
Ron (*joking*) What, are they out-of-season, clay pigeons then? (*He laughs*)
Janice Do people want more music or a bit of peace and quiet?
Barry Bit of quiet.
Pauline We have piped music on in the store now you know. I thought I'd hate it at first but you right get to like it after a time. Machine broke down yesterday, and honestly the silence . . . ! You wonder how we ever stood it!
Ron Fag anybody?
Pauline Thank you.
Janice Got one, ta.

Ron Barry? Fag?

Barry shakes his head

Pauline How is the arcade then, Barry?
Janice He's thinking of extending, aren't you? Building on.
Pauline Really.
Janice That's if he can get planning permission.
Pauline Oh.
Janice Not right keen on giving it, are they? How long did it take you to get permission to open? That took ages!
Ron I suppose it's these toffee-nosed councillors, is it? Think all amusement arcades centres of vice and drugs. Young girls waiting to be picked up and raped and . . . all that . . .

An unfortunate reference, as everyone, including Ron, is aware. He gives an embarrassed laugh

Pauline I see you've got some cards then, Jan.
Janice Yeah. Some folk never forget. Even when you want 'em to.
Pauline Go on. You're not that old.
Janice I'm not that young. (*She brings a card*) I got this from me dad.
Pauline Ah . . . ! And how is he?
Janice Oh, younger than me. Or you'd think so, way he carries on. He goes these great, long walks.
Ron He's still in that same place, is he? That old people's, er . . .
Janice Yeah. Never had it so good he says. There are three women to every man!

And they share a laugh

Pauline I think it's lovely when old people still, you know, take an interest.
Barry (*to Ron*) And how's your nice little number?
Ron (*not following*) My, er . . . ?
Barry Job.
Ron Oh . . . we're surviving. Heads above water.
Pauline Made some redundant though, haven't they.
Ron Production staff.
Barry But you're still roaming the streets?
Ron Oh yeah . . . yeah.
Janice (*to distract*) Pauline, let me get you another drink, love.
Pauline Well, just a small one then.
Ron No, you see, the less work they have on, the more they need their sales staff. I mean you cut your sales staff and you're cutting your own throat.
Barry You've still got that car then?

Ron hesitates, not clear what he means

Janice Course he's got his car! What do you think he does, goes round on a bicycle? He's not selling lavatory brushes you know!
Barry I know what he's not bloody selling! Belt up will you.
Janice (*to Pauline*) Listen. Way he talks to me.

Barry I'm asking him if he's got *same* car!

Janice Manners maketh man they say, don't they. Don't know what that makes him.

Barry Makes me tired of hearing you.

Janice Just oozes charm. I tell you, kid, after my husband Terry Wogan sounds dog-rough to me.

Barry For God's sake, woman . . .

Janice Ask me nicely! Just try asking me nicely for a change!

Barry Will you. Please. Shut your face.

Janice (*to Pauline*) You see. He can do it when he wants to.

Pauline Well, if you can't be yourself in your own home then where can you be.

Ron Still same car, yeah.

Barry Maroon Cortina.

Ron (*puzzled*) Yeah.

Janice D'you want its number? Are you collecting car numbers now? A new hobby is it on top of your swearing and getting pissed?

Barry Yeah.

Janice Oh well, I'll tell you where you'll get a lot. Go and stand in fast lane of th'M-six.

Pauline (*to Ron*) You're due for a new one though, aren't you.

Ron Well. I were a month or two back but . . . (*And a gesture: it hasn't happened yet*)

Pauline Another little economy.

Ron False economy.

Pauline Oh yes.

Ron You want to sell, you've got to turn up looking successful, not in a clapped-out Cortina. A V-reg nowadays, it's a right giveaway.

Barry Is it, yeah? A right giveaway is it?

Ron, surprised, hesitates. We hear the front door

Janice Hey.

We hear footsteps going up the stairs

(*Calling*) Alan . . . ?

The footsteps stop

Alan (*off*) Yeah.

Janice It's Alan.

Barry (*calling*) Come here!

Janice Back early isn't he? Didn't he say he was going to some speedway thing?

Alan reluctantly enters

Barry (*going to him*) All right?

Alan Yeah.

Janice Ron and Pauline are here.

Pauline Hello, Alan.

Ron All right?

Alan nods

Barry Nowt up is there?
Alan Naw, just . . . fed-up.
Barry Here. (*He takes out a wad of notes and starts peeling off a generous handful*)
Alan What?
Barry Your wages. Haven't given you 'em, have I.
Alan Oh.
Janice (*tutting*) Do you have to do that now?
Barry No, but I want to, don't I. (*He gives Alan the money*) There. And. (*Some extra*) A bonus. Productivity bonus.
Alan I haven't even been in.
Ron (*amused*) Must be good! Productivity bonus and he han't even been in!
Barry And spend it, eh. Have a good time.
Alan Yeah. Ta.
Ron I wish I worked for you!
Barry (*ignoring that; to Alan*) And you've not to bother, right?
Alan Yeah.
Barry 'Cause you've nowt to bother about. There's no way we're going to let 'em pin anything on you, right?
Janice (*a quiet warning*) All right, Barry.
Barry No way anybody is going to pin owt on my son.
Janice (*to Alan*) D'you want a drink? You can take it up to your room. You don't have to stop and talk to us.
Ron (*joking*) Teetotal is he? Signed the pledge?
Barry He's whatever he wants to be.
Alan See you then.
Barry So long son.

And Alan exits to upstairs, to "goodbyes" from Ron and Pauline

Pauline He's looking well anyway. I mean despite . . .
Janice (*to Barry*) Not like him to be in this early though, is it.
Barry (*as he helps himself to another drink and sits down*) What do you expect? You complain about what it's like for you. What the hell do you think it must be like for him!

To which Janice does not reply

Ron Terrible business.
Pauline Oh, it's awful. I don't know how you've stood it.
Janice Neither do I.
Pauline Anybody mentions a word about it to me, I say that family are my friends. I don't want to hear one thing said against that boy.
Janice Look, can I just say—I mean it is my birthday—can I just say that I'd rather we didn't talk about it. Just for tonight. Not talk about it at all.
Ron (*apologetic*) Oh . . .
Pauline Course we don't want to talk about it.

Ron Sorry, I weren't thinking ...

Janice I mean for five days now it's been nowt else. It's been police, newspapers ... I daren't even switch telly on. So I mean just for tonight I'd like to be able to forget about it.

Pauline And that's what we shall do.

Janice I mean you two were th'only two I wanted to see.

Pauline Ah ...!

Janice I just wanted to sit down, have a chat, summat to eat ... And even if nobody does like pizzas, I mean what the hell, we'll throw 'em away, go out and buy fish-and-chips ...!

Ron Hear, hear!

Pauline I thought you said you liked 'em ...?

Janice And—I'll warn you now—I'm going to get rather drunk. In fact more than rather drunk. I'm going to get rather pissed. So excuse me if I start to sing, dance, tell jokes ...

Pauline Or take your clothes off!

Janice Oh no! I'm not doing that again!

Pauline The Poco Poco had never seen anything like it!

Ron I'm sorry I missed that.

Janice I'm not. But I just feel I need, you know, a night off.

Pauline Course you do.

Janice Never mind all your Valiums and your sleeping-pills and your ... whatevers. I need a night wi' me friends when I can get pissed and nobody'll mention owt about ... you know, that that we're not mentioning owt about.

Pauline Right!

Ron I'll drink to that.

Janice It'll stop me moaning at him (*Barry*) as well, won't it, eh. (*She sits on the arm of his chair, becoming affectionate*) If I'm drinking it'll stop me moaning at you about what you're drinking!

Barry Doubt it.

Ron Well, I'd like to propose a toast. To Jan. A happy birthday and, er ...

Pauline Happy birthday, love.

Janice Ta.

Barry (*to Ron*) You knew her, didn't you. That girl.

A beat. Then Janice gives a moan of dismay, moves away from him

Janice Bloody marvellous ...

Ron What, the, er ...

Barry Her that were killed.

Janice Are you deaf or summat? Didn't you hear what I said? That I didn't want to talk about it!

Barry Nobody's asking you to.

Janice I don't want *anybody* to talk about it!

Pauline Oh dear.

Barry And we all have to do what you say, do we?

Janice Well it is my birthday, isn't it! I mean just for one night you might

show a bit of . . . of . . . oh, I dunno, it's that long sin' you've shown any I
can't remember what it is!

Pauline Consideration.

Janice Exactly.

Ron (*to Pauline*) Hey, you keep out of it.

Which draws a displeasing look

Barry She worked at your place, didn't she?

Ron Yes . . . yes.

Barry Yeah.

Janice All right? Satisfied now?

Barry Not really, no.

Ron Mind you, she'd left before . . . I mean she had left. I believe.

A pause. Barry stares at an increasingly uncomfortable Ron

Pauline Do you know, there was an advertisement in the newspaper for a
little like recorder thing that you fix to your fridge door so that whenever
you open it you get this voice that bursts out laughing. (*To Ron*) I showed
you, didn't I.

Ron Yeah.

Pauline Or you could get it to make comments like—"Don't say you're
eating again!" Or—"Why don't you try taking less ice with your drink?"
And then the laughing. I think you could get the comments and the
laughing as well. You see some amazing things advertised, don't you.

Janice You do.

Pauline There was another for a clock that ran backwards. (*To Ron*) I
showed you . . .

Ron You showed me.

Pauline Numbers were the wrong way round and the hands went back to
front. You had to be a mathematical genius to work out what time it was.
I always look at the adverts, what do you call 'em . . .

Ron Classified.

Pauline I think they're the most interesting part of a newspaper.

Barry gets to his feet and pours himself another drink

Janice Why don't you just get a straw and drink it out of bottle?

Barry Don't want to show you up.

Pauline There was another for a radio fitted into a cap. I think it was for if
you were riding a bike . . .

Ron (*stopping her*) Hey. All right, yeah.

Barry You like new things, do you, Pauline, eh?

Pauline (*at a loss*) New, er . . . ?

Barry And Ron? You like new things?

Janice What are you on about?

Barry Just conversation, my love. Just bloody silly conversation like you
wanted. (*To Ron*) No, I've got a new machine. Latest model.

Pauline Oh what, a sort of Space Invaders?

Barry Space Invaders, Pauline, are already part of history. We've moved on since them little buggers, by God we have.

Janice What's this called? Cosmetic summat or other ... ?

Barry Cosmic Raiders.

Janice That's it.

Barry Magic it is. At least it'd better be for what it's cost. (*To Ron*) Come on, I'll show you.

Ron Oh. Yeah, right ...

Pauline You're not going all the way to the arcade, are you?

Janice No, he has it set up in garage.

Ron See you later then.

Pauline Oh, the boys are going to play, are they.

Ron Looks like it.

Janice You have to be sober to play them things.

Barry and Ron exit through the kitchen to outside

(*With more resignation than anger*) He's a sod, in't he, my husband. I mean, be honest, Pauline, he's a sod and a half when he wants to be.

Pauline Well, I've never seen him like this.

Janice I have.

Pauline I mean with Ron. The way he's been behaving towards Ron ever since we got here.

Janice Oh, he's just . . . just mood he's in. D'you want a smoke?

Pauline Ta. Ron's run off wi' mine.

And they take and light a cigarette each

Janice These last ... how many ... four days. You can't imagine. God, I am going to get pissed! I deserve it! (*And she gets herself another drink*) You want one?

Pauline No, thank you.

Janice I've got so's I can't hardly go out. I'm scared to death of bumping into her parents. Amanda's. I mean what could I say?

Pauline shakes her head in sympathy

I'm like an hermit in here.

Pauline I can imagine.

Janice And what it must be doing to our Alan ... ! You don't know how lucky you are, not having children, Pauline, you don't!

Pauline No ... ?

There is an edge of bitterness to this which Janice, preoccupied with her own feelings, misses

Janice Suffering they bring you.

Pauline No, I've never seen Barry like that before.

Janice (*coming out of her reverie*) Oh, he can be a pig when he wants to be. He were a ... what-d'you-call-em ... a male chauvinist pig before they were fashionable, he were!

Pauline But he normally gets on wi' Ron.

Janice It's just ... mood he's in. And drink he's had.

Pauline (*persisting*) It were almost as though he were accusing Ron. You know. As though he knew something. Something that he didn't like.

Janice (*treading carefully*) No. Well not ... it's just ...

Pauline Just what?

Janice Oh look, Pauline, I'll tell you, but promise you won't tell Ron.

Pauline I knew there was something.

Janice Well, it's nowt. It's really nowt. But you know what men are like when they get a bee in their heads. Only he's that worried about Alan. 'Cause he thinks police might be trying to frame him. So he's been doing his own Sherlock Holmes bit. Asking around. Making enquiries.

Pauline What about?

Janice About who knew this Amanda girl. Just that. Who knew her.

Pauline And Ron knew her.

Janice Well, he helped her get her job, didn't he.

Pauline So I believe.

Janice So I mean he must have known her.

Pauline From what I hear there weren't many that didn't.

Janice Oh, I'm not, you know, suggesting owt ...

Pauline No.

Janice Only that he knew who she were, knew her to talk to.

Pauline Yes.

Janice That's all.

Pauline Well then, I'm sorry, Jan, but I still don't see it.

Janice See ... ?

Pauline Why Barry's like he is.

And she waits. Until Janice is pushed to admit

Janice Well. The other thing ...

Pauline Yes?

Janice You won't tell Ron, though, will you love? Last thing I'd want'd be to be causing trouble.

Pauline Jan, love, we were at school together, right? We were in Legion of Mary. You were my bridesmaid ...

Janice Oh I know ...

Pauline And I'd have been yours if you'd have been having any.

Janice I know.

Pauline Well then.

Janice (*hesitating, then*) You know newsagent's at th'end of road?

Pauline Yeah.

Janice Well, he's a right nosey get. And handling all them Sunday papers must have affected his brain 'cause he'll see bad in owt. Well, what's happened, he's noticed Ron's car ... I don't know how many times but ... th'odd afternoon he's noticed it parked out here in this road.

Pauline Ron's Cortina.

Janice Yeah.

Pauline That Barry were asking about.

Janice nods

I see. Well do go on.

Janice No, there's nowt else. Honest, love, that's all there is to it. Except that Barry's that . . . that worked up about everything, he's at stage where everything has to mean summat. Ron knew Amanda. Ron's car's been parked in this road . . .

Pauline So what does it mean?

Janice Well . . . nowt! Like I said . . . nowt!

Pauline Oh. Well, that's all right then.

Janice (*relieved*) You'll have another drink now?

Pauline Why not. After all, it's only your birthday once a year in't it.

Janice That's getting once too many an' all.

Pauline I must admit, though, there is just one little thing that I don't quite see. I mean I'm sure it's obvious and I just haven't thought of it. But what was Ron's car doing parked outside in your road?

Janice Could have been owt.

Pauline Must have been when he was calling here I suppose.

Janice I dunno, love, I don't honestly.

Pauline Well, what else? Unless Barry's right and he were helping that Amanda to a bit more than just a job.

Janice Oh no, Pauline, no, don't start thinking stuff like that!

Pauline Well . . .

Janice It must have been when he were calling here, yeah.

Pauline You think so?

Janice I know so. There's nowt for you to worry yourself about.

Pauline No . . . ?

Janice There isn't.

Pauline No. I mean if my husband's calling here in middle of th'afternoon it's no business of mine is it.

Janice (*looking at her, then*) Oh, Pauline, come on . . .

Pauline Yes? Come on what, Jan?

Janice Well! I mean you sound as though . . . as though you suspected me and Ron of having an affair or summat . . . ! (*And laughs*)

Pauline Well, I'll tell you one thing, shall I.

Janice What?

Pauline He's having an affair wi' somebody. I know that for a fact.

Janice Oh no . . . !

Pauline Oh yes.

Janice Oh Pauline, not your Ron. . . !

Pauline You don't have to patronize me, Jan.

Janice Well . . .

Pauline We're not in the Legion of Mary any more, either of us. And Ron never was. He'll chase anything in a skirt if he thinks there's half a chance of the skirt coming off.

Janice (*looking at her, then*) Well, thanks.

Pauline Don't mention it. Can I have another cigarette?

Janice Help yourself. I'm going to have another drink. I mean why not?

There's only me son being accused of murder and me being accused of having it off wi' me best friend's husband!

Pauline I'm not accusing. I'm only doing the same as your Barry.

Janice And what's that?

Pauline Putting two and two together. I mean I know Ron's having an affair wi' somebody and has been for a while. And the reason I know is that I know him and I know what it means when he's acting like he is.

Janice Well, I'm sorry to hear that, Pauline, I am. But I swear to God I don't know owt about it.

Pauline Barry thinks he does though, dun't he.

Janice (*looking at her, then*) What Barry's got into his thick head's to do wi' that poor little sod that were strangled on Sat'day night. It's nowt to do wi' me, love.

Pauline (*becoming tearful*) Oh, I don't know! I don't know what to think now . . .

Janice Oh love, come on, don't upset yourself . . .

Pauline Well.

Janice I mean, OK, 'appen Ron has called here th'odd time or two. So what though? We're all old friends, aren't we? Why shouldn't he call?

Pauline I suppose so.

Janice I mean this afternoon. He called this afternoon, right?

Pauline Yeah?

Janice Just to ask were it, you know, all right for you two still to come round, I mean wi' all that's happened and everything. Well, I mean 'appen frog-eyes at th'end of road saw him then as well. But so what eh?

But Pauline's suspicions are confirmed rather than dispersed

Pauline This afternoon?

Janice Yeah. I mean if you want all sordid details we had this really hot cup of coffee as well!

Pauline (*not amused*) So why did he act as though he hadn't seen you for ages?

Janice When?

Pauline When we were getting ready to come here. When we were in the car. It was all—I wonder how Jan is? I wonder how Jan's bearing up! As though he hadn't seen you for ages.

Janice (*hesitating then*) It must have been just . . . th'impression you got.

Pauline It was the impression I was meant to get.

Janice Look, Pauline, I swear. There's been nowt between us.

Pauline And I'm supposed to believe you, am I?

Janice Oh, for God's sake . . . !

Pauline See, I know you too well, Janice Clark! And you've always been the same. Anything you've taken a fancy to, you've had to have it. And, all right, you think your husband's a pig—which of course everybody knows that he is—so what's more natural than that you should start looking at other folks's? Starting wi' mine on account of us being such good pals!

Janice And don't you think I've got other things to think about? Don't you think I've got enough on my mind wi' all that's been going on around here?

Pauline I've never known your mind have much effect on what your body might be up to.

Janice You bitch! There's been my son down at the police-station for two days . . .

Pauline And there's been my husband round here by the sound of it!

Janice Your really believe it, don't you.

Pauline I'm not th'only one am I. I think that perhaps your Barry's come to the same conclusions that I have.

Janice All that Barry's worried about, Pauline, is our Alan and what cops are likely to do to him. And that's enough to be going on wi'. So just keep your daft ideas to yourself, will yer!

Pauline You're frightened of him finding out?

Janice There's nowt to find out! (*Then*) But you know what he's like. I mean think of risk I'd be taking having an affair wi' anybody! If Barry ever found out . . . I don't know what he'd do. He'd kill me.

Pauline Kill you, would he.

Janice He would. He'd bloody murder me!

A beat. As we hear the back door flung open

Pauline Like father like son then.

Janice stares at her. Then, before she can react:

>   *Barry staggers into the room. He has his hands crossed over his stomach. Sways. Stands looking at them through glazed eyes*

They stare at him, momentarily mesmerized by his sudden appearance and the condition that he appears to be in

Janice Barry . . . ?
Pauline Where's Ron?
Barry (*in pain*) Ron's in garage.
Janice What's up?
Pauline He's drunk.
Barry I'm not drunk.
Janice Well, you're giving a good impression. Sit down. I'll make you some black coffee or summat.

But, as Barry moves to sit down, he takes his hands away from his stomach. And reveals the blood staining the front of his shirt. Janice screams

Pauline Oh, my God . . .
Janice Barry! What've you done!
Barry 'S nowt . . . 's nowt . . .
Pauline (*in sudden panic*) Ron? Where's Ron? (*She calls*) Ron!
Ron (*off*) I'm here. I'm all right.
Janice Pauline, help me, what should we do?
Barry Bit of a cut, that's all . . .

Ron, white-faced, appears at the kitchen door

Ron It were an accident.
Pauline *You*'re all right?
Ron Yeah.

Barry gives a grunt of pain, then loses consciousness, slumps down. Janice screams

The hall door opens. Alan stands there, drawn downstairs by the noise

He'll want an ambulance.
Pauline (*to Alan*) Something's happened to your dad!
Janice Barry ... Barry ...
Pauline (*to Alan*) Don't just stand there! Ring for an ambulance!

Alan retreats into the hall to do so

Janice What do we do? Pauline, help me! What do we do?

Black-out

ACT II

Scene 1

The same. Three days later. Morning

The curtains are closed so that the R area of the room is gloomy in contrast to the daylight elsewhere. A coffin stands on trestles, the lid on, inside this darkened area. Beside it, a crucifix and candles (unlit) make a small altar. On the lounge side of the room the furniture has been moved back to create space. The dining-table has been moved and now supports cups and saucers

Janice, dressed for a funeral, enters from the kitchen. She is on edge, has been weeping. She carries a milk-jug and sugar-bowl which she places on the table. Then has a glance round the room. She removes a bottle of whisky that is too conveniently to hand and puts it away

Janice I'm not having 'em boozing here, I'm not. It'll be bad enough after, but I'm not having 'em standing at graveside breathing their fumes over him.

Alan enters from the kitchen. He is also dressed for a funeral. He carries a plate heaped with biscuits

And just make sure you behave yourself as well. You're taking your dad's place, remember. If there are any prayers in church—which there are bound to be—then you make sure you join in! And when everybody else kneels down, you kneel down. I don't want showing up, today of all days!

Through which Alan has stood unresponsive, holding his plate of biscuits

Well, put 'em down then!

Which he does. Then:

Come here.

She embraces him, puts her head on his shoulder. He stands, putting up with it rather than responding

I'm sorry, I'm going on at you, aren't I. My son. You're my son, you know that?
Alan Yeah.

She looks at him, scans his face as though seeking something familiar which is now gone, then gives up. She drops her arms from him and steps away

Janice Ah well. Soon be all over.

Alan Do you want me to do owt else?
Janice No.

So Alan moves to leave

Hey, where're you going?
Alan Nowhere.
Janice What d'you mean, nowhere? Where're you going that's nowhere?
Alan Just going upstairs, that's all.
Janice Well, why? We'll have folk starting to come in ten minutes. I mean, why d'you have to go upstairs? Why can't you stop in the same room as me for ten minutes?

Alan gives a long-suffering sigh and stays where he is

Today of all days. You're off up to your room like a scalded cat! Well, all right, go on then. Get off up to your blessed room!
Alan I'll stop here.
Janice You will not! No! If you haven't got enough ... enough natural feeling about you to want to stop off your own bat then I don't want you stopping on my account! I mean stop up there for funeral if you like! Why not? You'd stop up there if it were my funeral! You'd stop up there for mine, wouldn't you!

During which: Barry has appeared beside the coffin. He is wearing a long, white dressing-gown. He is pale-faced, sickly, walks slowly and with difficulty

Alan I'm stopping. All right? I'm stopping!
Janice (*looking at him, shaking her head*) I don't know. I sometimes think I don't know you any more. You might be somebody else's son, not mine.

Both of them notice Barry and turn in surprise

Good God in heaven ...
Alan Dad?
Barry Who d'you think it is.
Janice Scared me to death ...
Barry Scared meself to death when I looked in mirror.
Janice (*recovering; and concerned*) What're you doing? Just what d'you think you're doing down here? (*To Alan*) Help him. Help your dad to a chair!
Barry (*refusing the offer*) I've got legs of me own.
Janice Yeah, but you shouldn't be on 'em. What're you doing down here?
Barry (*reaching a chair and thankfully lowering himself into it*) Well, I can't get no peace up there wi' you two rowing.
Janice We're not rowing.
Barry No? You'll waken th'old feller (*in the coffin*) way you're going on. Never mind me.
Janice Barry, don't you think I've enough on me hands at moment wi'out you wandering about? You're supposed to be in bed. Doctor said you were to stop in bed!

Barry (*to Alan*) Get us a cup of tea, son, will yer.

Alan exits to the kitchen

Janice There'll be guests coming in a minute.
Barry So? They've seen me before.
Janice Not like this they haven't.
Barry Anyhow, I'm up now. Might as well pay me last respects to th'old feller.
Janice (*as she realizes*) Oh no ...
Barry What?
Janice Oh no, Barry, you're not thinking of coming to funeral ... ?
Barry Already here aren't I.
Janice But you're not going out. You're not going to that draughty church and then standing at side of that grave!
Barry Course I am.
Janice Oh, that's all I need. That is all I need!
Barry Good.
Janice We'll be burying you as well if you catch a chill on top of having had three inches of chisel in your stomach!
Barry I've never had a chill in me life.
Janice Never been stabbed before either.
Barry Listen. If it'll make you any happier, I'll stop in car at cemetery, right? Mind you ... where's dinner going to be?
Janice Co-op.
Barry Ay well, 'appen I can stand church and cemetery better than I can stand dinner at Co-op. I don't know whether me guts are up to that! (*And he laughs, then winces with pain*)
Janice You see.
Barry See what?
Janice State you're in.
Barry Haven't to laugh, that's all. So what better place to be than a funeral, eh? Won't be a lot of laughing there, will there.
Janice You look worse than me dad, you do honest.
Barry Ay well, his worries are over, aren't they.

Alan enters with a cup of tea

Cheers, son. And how're you?
Alan OK.
Barry Have you put sugar in?
Alan Yeah.

The doorbell rings

Janice Listen! They're here now!
Barry He'll go. (*To Alan*) And if it's th'undertaker, just make sure they take right feller, eh. I'm not ready for him yet.

Alan goes out to the hall

Janice I don't think that's right funny either.

Barry It weren't meant to be. It bloody kills me laughing does. I don't want anybody saying owt funny round here.

Janice tuts. They wait for the first of the mourners to arrive

Ron and Pauline enter, both momentarily taken aback at seeing Barry. Alan follows

Pauline Janice love ...
Janice Pauline ...

And they embrace

Ron All right love?
Janice Hello, Ron.
Pauline And how're you, Barry?
Barry Not so bad. Just a bit puffed from doing cartwheels, that's all.
Janice He shouldn't be out of bed.
Barry Oh, give up.
Ron You're, er, on the mend then ... ?
Barry (*nodding*) There's hope yet.
Ron I'm glad to hear it. And no, er, no hard feelings ... ?

And he offers his hand, which Barry takes

Barry I got nowt I didn't ask for.

At which Ron is relieved, as are Pauline and Janice

Pauline (*to Janice*) I wanted to come a bit early in case there were owt I could do.
Janice I think it's all done, love. (*Indicating Alan*) I had me helper you see.
Pauline (*To Alan*) Been helping your mam, have you?
Alan Not a lot.
Janice (*mildly*) Go on, get off up to your room then.

Alan goes out to the hall

(*To Pauline*) Come and help us brew up, eh.
Pauline Right, love.

They exit into the kitchen

Ron (*after a pause*) Well. Job is this in't it.
Barry One we could have done wi'out just now.
Ron Oh ay.
Barry Th'old bugger said he were going to last longer than any of us. So he were lying an' all.
Ron He were always as fit as a flea when I saw him.
Barry Oh ay, he were. Till he dropped down dead.
Ron (*offering a cigarette*) Smoking?
Barry Ay, go on. Be first I've had this, so don't be surprised if smoke comes out of th'hole in me guts.
Ron Still all stiched up then?

Barry (*nodding*) Like th'heel of an old sock.

Ron I, er, I still don't know what came over me.

Barry You had it to do. There were me as drunk as a skunk going to wring your neck.

Ron Funny though, I didn't realize what I were doing really. It weren't what they call calculated or owt.

Barry Weren't either of us doing much calculating. And I don't know what the hell I were trying to get you to say.

Ron I just picked up owt I could lay me hands on.

Barry Ay well, next time try and make it an hammer, will you. Be a damn sight less painful.

Ron laughs

Cops haven't been on to you again, have they?

Ron No.

Barry No. Once I'd come to long enough to say that it were an accident, they couldn't have cared less even if I'd snuffed it after that. They even seemed to have laid off our Alan for last day or two.

Ron Good.

Barry Haven't got anybody else yet though, have they.

Ron Not as I've heard.

Pauline enters from the kitchen

Pauline Ron.

Ron Yeah?

Pauline Jan wants to know do we want to, you know, have a look at her dad?

Ron Have a look ... ?

Pauline The lid isn't fastened down apparently. Do we want to have a look before the undertaker comes?

Ron (*not keen*) Do you want to?

Pauline I think I'd rather remember him as he were.

Ron (*seizing on that*) That's it. So would I.

Pauline Rather than as he is now.

Ron Yes.

Pauline nods and exits to the kitchen

She won't mind, will she?

Barry No. And he won't. He's well past minding, he is.

Ron I'm not that keen on funerals to tell you truth.

Barry I'm surprised they've caught on as they have.

And they share a little laugh

Still, there'll be a drink and a bit of nosh after. At least there will be for you buggers. I'm not allowed drink.

Ron No?

Barry I don't get a right lot of joy out of eating either. Though 'appen I won't be th'only one seeing as it's Co-op.

But Ron is preoccupied, still has something that he feels he must say

Ron I've been thinking about, you know, what that newsagent chap said about my car . . .
Barry (*dismissive*) Oh . . .
Ron No, I can understand that it sounded peculiar . . .
Barry (*joking*) Now don't get me going on that again. I'm in no fit state to attack anybody today!
Ron (*persevering*) I mean I can only think that it were th'odd times when I were calling here. Dropping summat off for Janice that Pauline's wanted her to have . . .
Barry Yeah, yeah . . .
Ron I mean I don't want you to have any sort of . . . lingering doubts.
Barry Lingering hole in me guts, that's all I've got.
Ron You're sure?
Barry Course I am.
Ron (*lightly: he can now joke about it*) I were a bit in two minds about coming round here this morning, tell you the truth.
Barry (*amused*) You thought I might have had a go at you again . . . ?
Ron Well . . .
Barry I haven't strength of a kitten. If I had a go at him in there (*the coffin*) I'd come off worsted!
Ron No, I just didn't know . . .
Barry I told Jan to tell you over phone. That you were to come over and be as though nowt had happened.
Ron Oh ay, she told Pauline, yeah.
Barry I got no more than I asked for. State I were in, I hate to think how you'd have ended up if you hadn't stopped me wi' summat!

Ron gives an uneasy smile

  Janice and Pauline enter from the kitchen, Pauline with a cup of tea for Ron

  Oh, hey up.
Pauline Cup of tea.
Ron Oh, ta.
Janice Look at you.
Barry I know. I can't go to your dad's funeral in me dressing-gown.
Janice I'd still rather you didn't go at all.
Barry Well, I am going. Now be told.
Janice (*to Pauline*) Doctor said he were to have a week off in bed. That on no account were he to stir out of that bed!
Barry (*to Ron*) District Nurse came. Wi' a bottle for me to pee into. I said it's a small neck has that bottle, love . . .
Janice Yes, all right.
Barry I said I don't want to get owt stuck, you know what I mean . . . ! (*And he laughs, then winces with pain*)
Janice There. Serves you right.
Pauline Everybody'll understand if you stop here, Barry. I mean you don't look in any fit state to me.

Janice He's not.
Barry I'm bloody going!

Janice exchanges a look with Pauline: what can she do?

Janice Well, you'd best put some clothes on then.
Barry Have I got a black tie?
Janice Not that I know of.
Barry What about that 'un I got married in?
Janice That's not black, that's navy blue! (*To Pauline*) As if anybody'd get married in a black tie!
Barry Shout our Alan. He can buy us one.
Janice What, now?
Barry Yeah.
Janice There's no time!
Barry Course there's time! He can go on his bike. (*He calls*) Alan!
Janice I had to force him to put them good trousers on. Now he's going to get 'em all covered in oil.
Barry Well, what d'you want me to do? Go wi' an open neck? Or go borrowing from neighbours? There's been a few black ties down this road past week or two.

Janice tuts but has no answer

(*To Ron*) Give our Alan a shout.
Ron (*going to the kitchen door; calling*) Alan! Can you come down here a minute!

As:

Pauline What time is the undertaker due?
Janice Half-eleven.
Pauline Oh well. If he goes to Burton's he should have time, shouldn't he?
Janice (*giving a small shrug of acceptance, then to Barry*) Still going to have to get dressed, aren't you.
Barry I'm going. (*He tries to raise himself from the chair, and fails*) I shouldn't have sat down. That were me only mistake.
Janice You see.
Ron Do you want a hand?
Barry Do I buggery. (*And with a painful effort, he finally stands*)

Alan appears at the kitchen door

Alan.
Alan Yeah?
Barry Do us a favour, son, will you. Get on your bike and go and get us a black tie.
Janice And mind your trousers.

The doorbell rings

(*To Barry*) They're here. And you in your dressing-gown.
Barry I know what I'm in.

Janice (*to Alan*) You'll be quick, won't you love. We don't want everybody waiting.

And she goes to answer the door

Barry You've got some money?
Alan Yeah.
Barry Black tie. You'll get one anywhere. 'Cept a fish-and-chip shop.

Janice, upset, returns

Janice Barry.
Barry What?

She indicates with a gesture of despair the person following her

Detective-Constable Curtiss enters

Oh Christ.
Curtiss Mr Clark. (*He nods at Ron and Pauline*)
Barry What the hell do you want?
Curtiss I want Alan.
Janice Oh no ...!
Barry Get out of here! Get out of my house!
Janice Barry ...! (*To Curtiss*) He's not well! He shouldn't be out of bed!
Curtiss I heard there'd been a bit of an accident.
Barry Be another if you don't shift yourself!
Curtiss Now, no bother, eh. All I want is Alan. With me. Down at the station.
Janice Oh, for pity's sake, not now, no ...!
Barry You're a bastard. You've waited, haven't you. Bloody waited!
Curtiss Been waiting for a lot of things.
Barry Jesus Christ, if I weren't in the state I'm in ...
Ron Easy, Barry lad ...
Janice You can't take him away now!
Ron (*to Curtiss*) You do know there's a funeral here this morning, don't you.

Which Curtiss did not. He looks round. He has been vaguely aware of something strange about the gathering but only now makes sense of it

Curtiss Funeral ...?
Barry Course he knows! That's reason he's come!
Janice They can't take him! (*To Curtiss*) We're going to bury his grandad!
Pauline Perhaps they didn't know.
Curtiss Hang on, hang on ...
Barry I'll hang one on you, copper!
Curtiss There's a funeral. From this house. This morning ...?
Janice Yes!
Ron Mrs Clark's father.
Barry (*hurrying as best he can,* R) Here! What d'you think this is? (*indicating the coffin*) Fucking table decoration?

Janice Oh my God . . .
Ron Hey Barry . . .
Pauline Oh goodness me . . .
Barry Come here! Come here! (*He struggles to remove the lid of the coffin*)
Ron Hey no . . .
Barry You want to have a look at th'old feller? See he's not having us all on, eh?
Janice Barry, don't!
Curtiss I don't think that'll be necessary, thank you.
Ron Barry, come on . . .
Barry Didn't know? Course he fucking knew!
Curtiss I didn't as a matter of fact, no.
Janice You're not touching that coffin anyway! There's nobody touching it!
Curtiss No call to on my account.

As Barry has returned to his chair

Pauline Perhaps he really didn't know . . .
Ron (*in agreement*) No.
Barry Lying bastard.
Ron Sit down, come on . . .
Curtiss And it's the lad's grandad is it?
Ron Yes.
Curtiss What time is it, the funeral?
Ron Half-eleven . . . ?

He looks to Janice for confirmation. She nods

Pauline And there's a dinner afterwards at the Co-op.
Curtiss (*hesitating, then*) Look, if I can get my Super to agree . . . (*To Alan*) Will you give me your word that you'll go nowhere but to this funeral and then . . . well, it's probably best if you come back here, to the house.
Barry (*exhausted and in pain after his effort*) Give him nowt.
Janice Barry, he'll have to!
Curtiss (*ignoring that*) I've got your word on that, have I Alan?
Alan Yeah.
Barry There'll be us solicitor here as well.
Curtiss He'll be welcome. But, like I say, I'll have to get my Super's say-so on this first.
Janice What d'you want him for anyway?
Curtiss Well, I think it's probably best if we leave all that till this afternoon.
Ron Yeah.
Janice But will you never leave off and let him alone?
Barry Like I've been telling you all along. If they couldn't pin it on anybody else then they'd be back. Well, they're bloody back, aren't they.
Janice Oh no . . .
Pauline (*consoling*) Jan . . .
Curtiss I'll go and check.

And he exits

Janice Alan.
Alan What?
Janice There is nowt, is there? There's nowt you haven't told us, is there?
Barry Course there isn't! For Christ's sake, woman, what the hell are you asking him, eh?
Janice Alan . . . ?
Barry We know there's nowt! We know it, right?

No response. He insists

   Right?
Janice Yeah.
Barry Right. So. Let's get the old feller buried. Here, son. Help us up them stairs, eh.

   And they go out together

Black-out

SCENE 2

The same. The afternoon of the same day

The coffin, with accompanying altar, etc., has now gone. The curtains have been opened and the room returned to normal

Janice sits alone in a chair, smoking a cigarette. She is nervous and ill-at-ease

   Pauline enters from the kitchen with a cup of tea for each of them

Pauline There we are.
Janice Ta.
Pauline Well. All over then.
Janice Me dad, yeah. (*i.e. But not my son*)
Pauline I thought Father Clayton spoke very well. You could have almost believed he'd known him. And there were some nice wreaths, weren't there. I suppose we might be doing wreaths next—there's no knowing— we seem to have a new line every other week!
Janice What are they waiting for?
Pauline What love?
Janice Them coppers, out there in that car.

Pauline shakes her head: she doesn't know

   Just sat there waiting!
Pauline (*crossing to the window*) I did think it was uncalled for, following us to the cemetery like that. And then to the Co-op. (*She looks out*) Still there, yes.
Janice I don't know what Alan thinks he's doing either.
Pauline Isn't he up in his . . .

Janice In his room! Yeah, I know! And what's he doing there at a time like this, eh?

Pauline Well . . .

Janice I'll tell you what he's doing. He's up there so that he dun't have to be down here wi' me!

Pauline Oh Jan . . .

Janice That's what he's doing.

A pause

Pauline Is the solicitor coming here or . . .

Janice He'll meet 'em at police-station.

There is a knock at the front door, which is then opened

Is that them?

Ron (*off, calling*) Only me.

Pauline (*relieved*) It's Ron.

Janice Ron . . .

Pauline It's only Ron.

Ron enters

We thought you were the police.

Ron No. They're out there though.

Pauline We know.

Ron Looked at me as though . . . well, just looked at me.

Pauline Did you arrange it? To get off?

Ron Yeah. Told 'em I wouldn't be in at all today so . . .

Pauline (*to Janice*) So we can both stop for as long as you like. No need for you to be left on your own, whatever happens.

Janice Not much fun for you though, is it.

Ron Where's Barry?

Pauline He's just gone for a lie-down. He's in no fit state . . .

Ron I know!

Pauline He shouldn't be on his feet. Never mind going to any police station.

Ron shrugs: there's nothing they can do about it

Janice Ron.

Ron Yes love?

Janice Will you call our Alan down here please.

Ron Yes, right . . .

He goes out to the hall

Pauline Perhaps Alan's . . . well, I mean perhaps he's frightened, do you think?

Janice No.

Pauline Oh.

Janice I'm the one that's frightened. Him, I don't know what he is.

Ron (*off*) Alan?

Alan (*off*) Yeah?

Ron (*off*) Can you come down here. Your mam wants you.

And Ron returns

He's coming.
Janice Thank you.
Pauline Do you want a biscuit or anything, Jan?

Janice shakes her head

No, it was very filling that lunch, wasn't it.
Ron (*at the window*) There's another car arrived. That, er . . . who was here before.
Janice Curtiss.
Ron He's here.

Alan enters. He has changed from his funeral clothes into his everyday ones

Janice What've you got changed for?

Alan looks at his clothes, shrugs

I said what have you got changed for? You must have noticed, them aren't same clothes that you had on before!
Alan Dun't matter, does it?
Janice Well, it wouldn't have done you any harm to have at least gone down there looking decent! And what have you been hiding for? As soon as we got back you were off upstairs!

Alan gives a long-suffering sigh, says nothing

Don't you want to talk to me? Is that it?
Pauline Now, Jan . . .
Janice Can't you even stand being in the same room as your own mother?
Pauline (*to Ron*) Can't you say something?
Ron What? (*And a gesture of helplessness*)
Janice Well?
Alan I don't mind.
Janice You don't mind . . .
Alan No.
Janice They're going to take you away for I don't know how long and that's all you can say? Well, I know one thing, Alan. I don't know what you did or didn't do on that night but I know one thing. You hate me, don't you?

Alan stands mute

Pauline Jan . . .
Janice You've just shut me right out! Well, all right, go on, do! And I'll shut you out as well! (*And she strikes him across the face with her open hand*)
Pauline Hey now, Jan, come on . . .
Janice (*quieter*) Well. I don't know what's happened to him but he's not the son I brought up, not any more he's not.

Barry enters, in his funeral attire. He is still shaky and weak

Barry So what is he then?

Janice turns in surprise, has no answer

You stupid bitch! You choose your moments, don't you, eh!
Pauline She's upset ...
Barry His own mother turning against him! That's all he needs is that!
Janice (*muttering*) Him that's turned against me.
Barry Ay, and not wi'out good cause either!
Janice What?
Barry If he knows you're not for him! If he knows that you're pointing the finger along with the rest of 'em!
Janice I never said that.
Pauline No, she hasn't.
Barry Dun't have to be said. He can see it. Feel it.
Pauline Barry, how can you say a thing like that?
Barry 'Cause *I* can feel it. It's like fucking scent coming off her.
Ron (*at the window*) You've got visitors.
Barry Made their minds up have they.

The doorbell rings

(*To Janice*) Let 'em in.
Pauline Shall I go ... ?
Barry She'll go.
Janice I'm going.

Janice goes out

Barry (*putting a hand on Alan's shoulder*) All right son.
Alan Yeah.
Barry So am I.

Janice leads in Constable Curtiss

Curtiss Well then, Alan. I've waited as long as I can.
Barry Ay, we've seen you. Like vultures.
Curtiss Oh now be fair, Mr Clark ...
Barry Fair? What's so bloody fair about way you're persecuting him? Coming back time and again! And don't think I don't know why either!
Curtiss Oh?
Barry You missed me over that drugs business so now you're going to get him, right?
Curtiss (*dismissive*) Oh ...
Barry Oh yeah! And I'll tell you summat else as well. I'm coming down wi' him.
Curtiss (*hesitating, then*) Suit yourself. Might be a long wait though ...
Janice But why do you want him again? There's not summat new is there?
Curtiss There is, yes. We've had a witness come forward.

Janice Witness ... ?
Barry Lying bastard.
Curtiss (*to Alan*) Right, come on.

Janice hurries to embrace Alan

Janice Oh, my lad ...
Alan I'll be all right.

And Janice moves away from him and is comforted by Pauline

Barry I'll buy some fucking witnesses an' all. Get a hundred of 'em off dole
queue at ten quid a time!
Ron Good luck, lad.

   Curtiss escorts Alan out

Barry (*to Ron*) You're stopping here ... ?
Ron Yeah. We won't leave her.
Barry Cheers.
Janice Barry?
Barry What?

*But she can't put it into words. About her love for the two of them. Something
of which nevertheless gets over to him*

   I'll see he's all right.

   And, as best he can, he hurries out after them. The front door closes

Pauline (*to Janice*) Come on now. You're going to have a lie-down.
Janice Oh no ...
Pauline Yes! Yes, Jan, you are. You were exhausted with your dad's
funeral, never mind this.
Ron Yeah.
Pauline Barry's not going to be back for a long while yet.
Janice (*giving in*) Well, just an hour then. But you've to let me know
straightaway if you hear ...
Pauline We will, yes. Now, come on, I'll come up with you.
Janice I'll manage. It's Barry that's poorly, not me.
Pauline Well, just let me see you up the stairs then.

   They exit to the hall

*Left alone, Ron betrays a restlessness which he has up to now been hiding. He
shakes his head, paces the room, as if in despair. Then conducts a search for
the whisky bottle and, finding it, pours himself a large one*

   Pauline returns, and closes the door behind her

Pauline She's got more tablets up there than most chemists' shops.
Ron Christ, Pauline.
Pauline What?
Ron Stuck now, aren't we? Of all bloody places to be, we have to be stuck
here!

Pauline So?

Ron So . . . !

Pauline All right, all right, keep your voice down.

Ron I mean, suppose they tell him?

Pauline They won't though, will they.

Ron Well, suppose he finds out anyway—and don't ask me how 'cause I don't know—but suppose he just does—he finds out that their witness, their precious, bloody witness—that it's me.

Pauline He won't.

Ron He'd kill me. You know that? I'd be dead.

Pauline Don't be ridiculous.

Ron Ha!

Pauline And, anyway, they've only got a case so long as they've got you as a witness.

Ron Precisely.

Pauline And you've told them that you'll only testify so long as they don't tell him it's you.

Ron Can't do that forever though, can they.

Pauline For now.

Ron Can't do that at trial. You can't have an anonymous bloody witness at a trial!

Pauline So, all right, you get police protection. They promised you that, police protection.

Ron Oh great, yeah. So I have to go round arm-in-arm wi' a copper for rest of me life, do I!

Pauline Not for the rest of your life, no. And so what if you did? You're frightened it might cramp your style, is that it?

Ron (*not following*) What?

Pauline Stop you calling on your lady friends all day. Make you spend your time doing what you're supposed to be doing!

Ron (*a groan of despair*) Oh God . . .

Pauline Yes, I can see it might be an inconvenience having a policeman with you, I can!

Ron (*nodding*) What this is really about.

Pauline What?

Ron Never mind.

Pauline I do mind! You said that that's what this was really about.

Ron It is.

Pauline And would you care to explain what you mean by that, please?

Ron (*sighing, then*) You got it into your stupid head that I'd been having it off wi' Jan.

Pauline Still have it in my stupid head as well.

Ron So—like a fool—I told you about Amanda. Me and Amanda.

Pauline Hoping it'd make me forget about Janice.

Ron Then you make me go to police. And we know why, don't we.

Pauline Do we?

Ron As a way of getting back at Jan, that's bloody why!

Pauline Life isn't long enough for me to get my own back on all the women in this town that you've been knocking off.

Ron They've not all been your best friend though have they.

Pauline No. And they've not all had a son that's committed murder either.

A pause. Ron shakes his head. Gives up. But Pauline has not yet finished

And that girl.

Ron groans: not again!

That cheap slut of a girl.

Ron She does happen to be dead. In case you'd forgotten.

Pauline I haven't forgotten, no.

Ron Well then.

Pauline I haven't forgotten that she was pregnant by you when she died either. And I don't suppose I ever will.

Ron No.

Pauline I mean what did you see in a girl like that, a girl half your age . . . ?

Ron I've told you.

Pauline You've told me nothing.

Ron (*goading her*) Pure sexual attraction. Pure, unadulterated, sexual——

Pauline (*stopping him*) Yes, all right.

Ron And if you can't understand that . . . well, all right, perhaps you can't, no.

Pauline I suppose she felt she was under an obligation since you'd helped her get her job.

Ron Did she.

Pauline Obvious isn't it. I mean why did she leave if it wasn't to get away from you?

Ron She left. Just left. Kids at that age, they get fed-up easily.

Pauline They get fed-up of being molested by men old enough to be their fathers!

Ron (*looking at her, then*) I think, you know, that you want to get some things clear in your head. It's Alan that took her down that alley. Alan that did any molesting that were done. Not me.

Pauline You weren't too far away though.

Ron (*nodding*) At a guess about . . . fifty yards. (*Then bitterly*) God, I must have been out of my head!

Pauline Yes.

Ron I mean letting you persuade me . . . nag me . . . humiliate me into going to the cops!

Pauline It was your own conscience that made you go.

Ron It sounded a lot like you then.

Pauline Well, don't you think you've a duty—I mean if he killed her, if he did it—don't you think you've a duty to speak up?

Ron Why?

Pauline Why? 'Cause she were a young girl. And he strangled her. That's why.

Ron She were a cheap slut two minutes ago. (*Then*) I mean it's not going to bring her back, is it?

Pauline Course it's not.

Ron It's going to ruin his life as well. Alan's. To say nowt of Barry's and Janice's. Not going to do us a lot of good either.

Pauline And so suppose you'd said nothing? I mean what he's done once he could do again.

Ron (*unconvinced*) Oh . . .

Pauline You don't think so?

Ron I don't think there were owt, you know, premeditated about it. Just one of them things.

Pauline One of them murders, yeah.

Ron You know what I mean. I mean he's not a bad lad. (*Then, before Pauline can protest*) I mean if you hadn't known about this then you'd have said that he weren't a bad lad.

Pauline And I'd have been wrong.

Ron She led him on. Be all accounts she led him on. Then probably changed her mind. Took the goods out of the winder.

Pauline And that excuses it, does it?

Ron No.

Pauline That makes it all right?

Ron shakes his head, gives up. Gets himself another drink, tries to settle, can't, wanders about the room

Pauline goes out to the foot of the stairs, where she listens for a moment, then returns

No sound from her anyway.

A further silence between them, then:

Ron And suppose they find him not guilty?

Pauline How can they?

Ron (*shrugging, he doesn't know*) Suppose.

Pauline They're not going to do, are they. You said that the police were sure that he's guilty.

Ron Yeah, but a jury might not be. Twelve average . . . thick as pig-shit most of 'em.

Pauline Then they'll believe the police, won't they.

Ron (*following his own train of thought*) Suppose his defence is that he just found her there after she'd already been killed be somebody else? Suppose he says that he's on his way home, he goes for a walk round, sees the body, picks her up, finds she's dead. So he puts her down again and leaves her there.

Pauline Rubbish.

Ron Why?

Pauline So why didn't he tell somebody?

Ron Because . . . 'cause he was scared.

Pauline All right, well later on then. When he'd been taken to the police-station. I mean he was supposed to have been there for about two days. Why didn't he tell them that then?

Ron Still scared.

Pauline (*protesting*) Oh ...

Ron He thinks if he changes his story then it'll make 'em suspect him all the more.

Pauline Can't suspect him any more than they do, can they.

Ron Anyway, listen. All I'm saying is, if—for one reason or another, never mind that—but if they decide he didn't do it, then you know who that leaves well and truly in the shit, don't you!

Pauline I suppose you're going to say you. But I don't see why.

Ron I was there! I mean I've gone and told 'em I was there! And, what's more, I had a motive.

Pauline What motive?

Ron Well, you're the one who keeps reminding me ...

Pauline (*realizing*) Oh ...

Ron She was pregnant.

Pauline Yes.

Ron By me. Or so she said. By a married man who therefore had good reason for wanting to keep her mouth shut!

A pause

Pauline Tell me, Ron. Tell me honestly.

Ron What?

Pauline Did you go near her at all that night?

Ron No!

Pauline Right then.

Ron Course I didn't. I didn't even know who it were, did I.

Pauline Well then there'll be no ... forensic ...

Ron Forensic evidence.

Pauline Right. They can't possibly accuse you of anything.

Ron They'll start wondering though, won't they.

Pauline Well. (*i.e. Nothing to be done about that*)

Ron Everybody will. Neighbours, everybody! I tell you, when this is over we're going to fucking Australia!

A pause. They both take and light cigarettes

Pauline Just tell me what you've told the police.

Ron I've told you.

Pauline That girl Amanda, she phoned you. You told them that?

Ron Yeah.

Pauline And ...?

Ron And she said she was pregnant and I was the father and what was I going to do about it? (*Then he corrects himself*) Well she didn't say that, no. She said she wanted to talk to me about it.

Pauline And you asked her when.

Ron (*nodding*) And she said then. That night. I had to go and see her there and then.

Pauline So you concocted a cock-and-bull story for me to explain why you had to go dashing out of the house at half-past eleven on a Saturday night. I mean I can collaborate all that.

Ron You're my wife.

Pauline So?

Ron I don't think it counts.

Pauline Well, it can't do any harm. So. Then what did you tell 'em?

Ron Well, she said that she'd just come back from a disco. Her parents were out, there was nobody in the house, she was all upset about having this kid and wanted to talk.

Pauline (*prompting*) So you drove round . . .

Ron Drove round here. She said she'd be waiting outside. Only . . . no sign of her. No lights on in the house either. So I didn't know what to do. I didn't want to park.

Pauline In case Janice noticed the car.

Ron Or Barry, yeah. So I drove round. Round this block. Then I noticed that there was somebody down that alleyway at the end. And I thought it might have been Amanda. I mean perhaps she'd decided to wait there where nobody'd see her. So I stopped. Then I saw it wasn't Amanda.

Pauline It was Alan.

Ron (*nodding*) Alan, yeah. And he was bending over this body. Touching it. And then he straightened up, looked round, and then he ran off. Down the other way. So I . . . I drove off.

Pauline And you're sure it was Alan?

Ron nods

I mean it was dark. This is what they're going to say. It was dark.

Ron There are street lamps. Was a light night anyway.

Pauline So you're sure it was him?

Ron (*nodding*) Wish I weren't.

Pauline And they're going to want to know about what he was doing, aren't they. I mean you said he was touching her . . .

Ron Yeah.

Pauline Well how, I mean . . .

Ron (*shaking his head*) Just . . . had his hands on her. I mean it was about, what, forty, fifty yards away . . .

Pauline Well, all right. But it was him. So long as we know it was him then you're doing your duty telling 'em that.

Ron Yeah.

Pauline Nobody can criticize you for that. You're just following the dictates of your own conscience.

Ron (*bitterly amused*) That's what I'm doing is it . . . !

Pauline And whatever happens now . . . well, it's going to happen, isn't it. It's not something anybody can blame you for.

Black-out

SCENE 3

The same. The evening of the same day

The curtains are closed, lights on. Ron has fallen asleep in his chair. Pauline is glancing through a magazine. Janice is sitting staring blankly ahead. She is wearing a dressing-gown. Cups, ashtrays, etc. all testify to the length of time they have been waiting

A long pause. Ron begins to snore

Pauline Ron.
Ron (*awakening*) Eh ... what ... ?
Pauline You were snoring.
Ron Oh ... sorry ... sorry.

Another pause. Then Janice sits up, suddenly alert

Pauline What is it, love?
Janice He's here.
Pauline (*looking to Ron*) I didn't hear ...

Ron shakes his head: he didn't hear either. Then the front door is opened

Janice Oh God.

   The wait for Barry to enter is a fraction longer than they, and we, expect. When he does appear, he is white and drawn, moving slowly, physically at the end of his tether

   Barry ... ?
Ron All right ... ?
Pauline Help him then!

Which Ron hurries to do

Barry 'S all right ...

But he allows Ron to assist him to a chair

Janice Well, what's happened, Barry? What's happened to our Alan?

He does not reply, still recovering from the effort of his journey

Ron Can I get you owt?
Barry Get us a whisky.
Pauline Is that wise? I mean considering ...
Ron (*getting it*) If it's what he wants, yeah.
Janice (*desperate*) For Christ's sake, tell us, will you.
Pauline Now, Jan, give him a chance to come to.

Barry takes the whisky from Ron, downs it in one, coughs and grunts at the shock of it

Barry Shit. (*He gives Ron the empty glass*) Get us another.

Which Ron does

Janice Have they charged him, Barry, have they? Just tell us that, will yer!

Barry looks at her. His manner is uncharacteristically low-key, defeated

Barry They have, yeah.
Janice Charged him wi' it?
Barry Yeah.
Janice Oh Christ Almighty . . . !
Pauline Oh no.
Ron (*with the whisky*) There. Get that down you.
Janice They've charged him wi' murder? They've charged our Alan wi' murdering that girl?
Barry It's what you expected, in't it.
Janice Expected . . . ? It's what I were frightened of, what I were scared to death of, if that's what you mean.
Pauline Now Jan . . .
Janice Oh, what're we going to do? God in heaven, what're we going to do!
Pauline Be brave, love, come on . . .
Barry Nowt to do.
Ron Is it that, er . . . that witness that's done it, is it?
Barry Eh?
Ron That witness . . . that they said . . .

But to Ron's surprise, Barry shakes his head

   No . . . ?
Barry Don't even know who the sod is.
Ron Oh.
Barry Served his purpose though.
Janice And what does the solicitor say?
Barry Not a lot. He reckons . . .
Janice (*over him*) He's bloody useless! (*To Pauline*) He's only a young lad, only about thirty! (*To Barry*) I said he were no good from start. There must be somebody else. We must be able to get somebody better, Barry!
Barry (*waiting for her to finish, then*) He reckons there's a chance they might settle for manslaughter.

A moment as they take this in

Janice Manslaughter . . .
Pauline Oh.
Barry What he reckons.
Janice Well, and whose side is he on? That'd still mean he were guilty, wouldn't it? Still mean that he killed her!
Ron It is less though.
Janice We want somebody that's on his side. That believes he's innocent!
Barry No chance.

They look at him

He's confessed.
Janice No.
Barry He killed her. He did it.
Janice Oh no, no! They must have made him say it, they must have made him! (*Turning on Barry*) I thought you were going to look after him!

Barry sits mute

Pauline Jan, I'm sure Barry's done all he could.
Janice Well, it weren't enough then, were it!
Pauline Now, come on ...
Ron (*to Barry*) It's, er, definite then, is it?
Barry (*nodding*) He's made a statement. Telling how he killed her.
Janice No.
Barry And signed it. Of his own free will.
Janice No.
Barry (*shouting*) Yes! Now shut it, will you! (*Then quieter*) He's made a statement. I've seen it. Read it. And if I can believe it, then I'm bloody sure you can.

Janice gives a little whimper of terror

Ron Poor lad.
Barry He were crying. Just crying. He wouldn't talk to me. Wouldn't look at me.

At which Janice finally breaks down, begins to weep uncontrollably

Pauline Oh love ...
Barry Take her upstairs.
Janice No ...
Barry Go on. Take her up.
Pauline Yes, come on, love. There's nothing more you can do ...
Barry You'll stop wi' her, won't you, Pauline.
Pauline I will.
Ron She will.
Pauline (*to Janice*) Come on, love, you're going to have a lot to face tomorrow ...
Barry You stop wi' her.

Pauline and Janice exit upstairs

Barry struggles to stand

Ron All right?
Barry Just help us off wi' this coat, will you.
Ron Yeah, sure ...

And he removes Barry's coat. Barry sits down again

Barry And get us another one of them. (*Meaning whisky*)
Ron Yeah. I'll have one meself if you don't mind while I'm about it. Well. I am sorry, Barry, I am. And for the lad I mean. Jesus.

Barry He's dead. Finished. Eighteen years old and his life's finished.
Ron Nay . . .
Barry His whole life.
Ron If it's manslaughter though, I mean . . . it might not be . . . that bad.
Barry I were ready to do owt. Give owt. Then they told me. He'd made this
statement. Saying he'd killed her. He'd put his hands on her throat and
strangled the cheap little tart.
Ron (*offering him a cigarette*) You want a . . . ?

Barry shakes his head, refusing it

I mean there's his age and that. They might, er . . .
Barry His mother knew, didn't she. She knew all right.
Ron Oh, I don't think . . . no.
Barry Even that sodding copper looked sorry for me. Even that bastard.
Ron It's a tragedy. It's a bloody tragedy, it is.
Barry He'd had it bang to rights all along that copper.
Ron And this, er, this witness . . .
Barry What about him?
Ron Well, were that, er, what swung it like?
Barry (*shrugging*) Some feller in his car. Passing. Reckons he more or less
saw it. Course I weren't having any of it. How much are you paying him I
said. What were he, an off-duty copper? Then solicitor came out. Wi' a
copy of his statement. Showed it me.
Ron So you don't even know who this witness were?
Barry (*shaking his head: he doesn't care*) Who needs him? Witnesses,
evidence . . . All beside the sodding point now, in't it!
Ron Yeah, I suppose . . . yeah.
Barry He's written it all down. Like a story it is.
Ron Yeah?
Barry He met her at that disco. She wanted to talk to him. So they go for a
walk. And she tells him she's pregnant.
Ron Oh.
Barry Not by him though.
Ron No?
Barry No. She wouldn't say who. So they have their walk. Go back inside.
Ron Yeah.
Barry Then, late on—his mates have gone off wi' some scrubbers—he sets
off home be himself. Gets as far as th'end of this road. And there she is,
this stupid tart, she's out there, hanging about, waiting for him. Well,
waiting for somebody anyway. And he's first that turns up.
Ron I see.
Barry So they start talking again. And she starts chatting him up, asking
him if he dun't fancy her. Well, I mean, Christ, he's eighteen. I mean you
fancy holes in trees at eighteen. So she says come into the house she says.
Her house. There's nobody in she says. But he won't. Says no. So she says
well let's go for a walk. Let's go down the lane there. So he goes wi' her
down the lane. (*Then*) It's like a story. You read it. It's like a kid's story.

Ron nods in sympathy. There is a pause as Barry seems lost in thought. Then suddenly:

Can you get summat for me?
Ron What? I mean yeah, yeah . . .
Barry (*struggling to produce a bunch of keys*) Out in garage.
Ron What is it?
Barry Oh, it's just a case. Brown leather case.
Ron Yeah?
Barry Only it's locked up. As you go in, there's like a cupboard. It's red, painted red.
Ron Yeah. (*He remembers it*)
Barry You want that key to open it. Then inside you'll see this brown leather case.
Ron (*taking the key*) You want me to bring it . . . ?
Barry (*nodding*) Bring it here.
Ron Yeah, right.

Ron goes out through the kitchen

Barry listens until he is sure that Ron is out of the house, then, with a supreme effort, lifts himself out of his chair. And, as quickly as he can he drags himself across to the sideboard, in which he opens a drawer. He takes from it a metal box. There is a combination lock on this. It takes him a moment to line up the numbers, then the lid is opened. He takes from it two small items which we cannot identify and places them in his pocket, then closes the box, replaces it in the drawer and, now desperate as his strength fails him, drags himself back to his seat. He collapses into it

Ron returns, carrying the leather case. He looks worried, uneasy

Barry (*still recovering*) Found it . . . ?
Ron Yeah. (*He puts the case down well out of Barry's reach and goes to him with the keys*)
Barry (*taking the keys*) Ta.
Ron (*noticing his condition*) You all right?
Barry (*nodding*) Just tried standing up. Shouldn't have done, that's all. (*Then he indicates the case*) Well, er . . . ? (*i.e. Can I have it?*)
Ron Look, Barry mate . . . (*And he shakes his head*)
Barry What?
Ron I opened it. That case.
Barry Yeah.
Ron Well, I mean . . . I know what's in it.
Barry So do I. So what?
Ron It's your gun.
Barry Yeah.
Ron Come on. (*i.e. You can't be serious*)
Barry Just give it us, Ron, eh.
Ron You're not . . . thinking of doing owt daft . . . ?
Barry No. There nowt daft about what I'm going to do.

Ron I'm not going to let you, you know. You think I'm going to give you that and then walk out and . . . (*He shakes his head*) No way, mate. No way.

Barry Look, I just want it. I just need to know it's there.

Ron What for though?

Barry 'Cause I do. Look, if I were going to top meself then all I'd have to do 'd be try and run up a flight of stairs. I'd be dead be I got to third step.

Ron It's got no cartridges wi' it.

Barry Right. So, what do you think I'm going to do, use it to bash meself over th'head? Give it here.

Ron decides, brings it and gives it to Barry

I just like it. Maybe I'm soft in the head. Maybe I've been soft in the head for a long time.

Ron I'm not leaving you wi' it. I'm telling you. I'm not going out of this room and leaving you wi' it.

Barry (*taking out the gun, handling it*) Been a while sin' I've used this you know. Too much work. Not enough time.

Ron I know the problem.

Barry You ever done any?

Ron Done . . . ? (*Then*) Oh no, not shooting, no.

Barry You stand, there wi' your gun. Shout to let 'em know you're ready.

Ron Yeah?

Barry Then up it comes. (*He tries to swing the gun up, finds it heavy*) Christ, I can hardly lift it!

Ron No, well . . .

Barry But it's all . . . all in speed. Not like target shooting where you can spend half-a-sodding-hour lining it up. This is all split seconds. You say the word—it's up—aim—and you've blasted the bugger.

Ron (*encouraged by Barry's talk*) You want to take it up again.

Barry 'Appen I will.

Ron Yeah.

Barry Anyhow. Didn't finish story, did I.

Ron What?

Barry Our Alan's statement.

Ron Well . . . no need is there.

Barry See, he went down th'alleyway wi' her. Just down far enough. Then she starts sticking her hand in his pocket. See if she can't bring him round to her way of thinking.

Ron Yeah well, it'll all sort of be in his favour, won't it.

Barry Only he still says no. Now I wouldn't have. And you wouldn't have, would you?

Ron gives an uneasy laugh

But Alan says no. And you know why?

Ron Well, er . . .

Barry 'Cause his mother's warned him. Don't touch her. She might have diseases. She has a reputation. If you don't catch her diseases, you'll catch

her reputation. And he listens to that sort of thing does Alan. Takes
notice of his mother.

Ron Yeah.

Barry Only she doesn't like that, the little tart. Seems she might be easily
pulled but she's easily offended as well. And if she's making offers then
she expects 'em to be taken up. So she starts mouthing off at him. Giving
him some choice mouthfuls on what she thinks about somebody who
dun't want to screw her.

Ron I see.

*Barry looks at him for a moment. Then puts his hand in his pocket and takes
out two cartridges — the two which he has earlier taken from the sideboard.
Ron stares at him, alarmed, though not yet alarmed for himself*

Hey, Barry ...

Barry And then do you know what she said?

Ron Them's cartridges ... ! What do you think you're doing, eh?

Barry Stop there!

Ron Hey, no ...

Barry And listen! I haven't finished me story yet.

Ron (*shouting*) Jan! Janice!

Barry Ay, all right, let's have her here as well. Why not. But you stop there.

Ron Come on, Barry ... what're you going to do wi' that gun, eh?

Janice and Pauline enter

Ron nods towards Barry. They stare at the gun

Janice What's he doing?

Pauline It's his gun.

Ron Why I shouted.

Janice What the hell're you doing?

Barry Listen!

Pauline Is it ...

Ron Loaded, yeah.

Barry Listen! I'm telling you why—why he killed her.

Janice You what?

Barry What she said made him grab her. Made him want to do owt to shut
her up!

Janice What?

Barry When he wouldn't give her what she wanted. What she said. She
said—he weren't as randy as his mother. Didn't have his mother's
fondness for it.

Janice (*quietly*) Oh no ... no, Barry ...

Barry You see, living over road, out of work for past two months, she's had
a lot of time on her hands, Amanda has. Time to watch from her window
and see all that's been going on.

Ron Hey no ...

Janice She'd seen ... ?

Barry (*nodding*) Seen what you two were up to, yeah.

Ron No, Barry, I swear . . . no, she'd got it all wrong . . . hadn't she, Jan? All
    wrong that!
Janice And that's why he killed her?
Barry Why he did for her, yeah. Stop her going on about his mother's dirty
    ways. Stop her telling tales. That's why he grabbed her round the throat
    and squeezed. And now his own life's wasted. Finished.
Pauline He's going to shoot us all.
Ron No, Barry . . . please . . . please . . .

*Pauline panics and rushes at Barry, who fires. The shot catches Ron in the
chest and he falls backwards. Pauline screams and rushes to him. Barry points
the gun at Janice, who stands acquiescing in her fate*

Janice Shoot me.

*He holds the gun pointing at her for a moment, then lets it fall. He starts to
sob. She puts out a hand. He takes it*

The Lights fade to Black-out

FURNITURE AND PROPERTY LIST

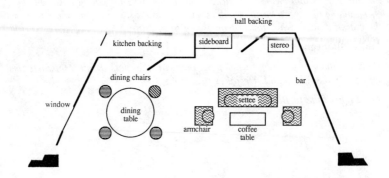

ACT I

SCENE 1

On stage: Settee
Armchairs
Coffee table. *On it:* ashtray, cigarettes, lighter, ornaments, 2 mugs of coffee
Bar. *On it:* glasses, bottles of drink including whisky, beer
Stacked stereo unit. *Beside it:* records, tapes
Sideboard. *On it:* table lamp, ornaments, birthday cards, sympathy card.
  In drawer: metal box with combination lock containing 2 cartridges (for
  II, 3)
Dining-table
Chairs
On walls: picture of Sacred Heart, crucifix, family photographs
Carpet
Window curtains (*open*)

Personal: **Janice:** lighted cigarette
Ron: lighted cigarette, cigarettes, lighter, wrist-watch (last 3 items required
  throughout)

SCENE 2

Strike: Dirty coffee mugs

Set: Window curtains closed
             Bowls of crisps, nuts on coffee table
             Drinks for **Barry**, **Janice**, **Ron** and **Pauline**

Off stage: Bloodstains on shirt **(Barry)**

Personal: **Barry:** wad of money in pocket

ACT II

SCENE 1

Strike: Dirty glasses and ashtrays
             Bowls of nuts, crisps

Set: Tidy bar, leaving bottle of whisky out
             Window curtains closed
             Coffin on trestles in dining area
             Crucifix and candles beside coffin
             Dining-table in lounge area. *On it:* cups and saucers
             Other furniture in lounge moved back to create space
             Clean ashtrays

Off stage: Milk-jug, sugar-bowl **(Janice)**
             Plate of biscuits **(Alan)**
             Cup of tea **(Alan)**
             Cup of tea **(Pauline)**

SCENE2

Strike: Coffin, trestles, candles, crucifix
             Cups, saucers, milk-jug, sugar-bowl, biscuits from table
             Dirty cups and saucers

Set: Window curtains open
             Furniture moved back to original positions

Off stage: 2 cups of tea **(Pauline)**

Personal: **Janice:** lighted cigarette

SCENE 3

Set: More dirty cups, saucers, glasses, dirty ashtrays, packets of cigarettes on
                coffee table
             Window curtains closed
             Magazine for **Pauline**

Off stage: Leather case containing shotgun **(Ron)**

Personal: **Barry:** bunch of keys in pocket

LIGHTING PLOT

Property fittings required: pendant light, table lamp

Interior. A through lounge. The same scene throughout

ACT I, SCENE 1.   AFTERNOON

To open: General interior lighting; table lamp on

Cue 1	**Barry**, still dissatisfied, takes another drink	(Page 17)
	Fade to black-out	

ACT I, SCENE 2.   Evening

To open: Pendant, table lamp on

Cue 2	**Janice:** "What do we do?"	(Page 30)
	Black out	

ACT II, SCENE 1.   Morning

To open: Gloomy lighting in dining area; daylight in rest of lounge

Cue 3	**Barry** and **Alan** go out together	(Page 40)
	Black-out	

ACT II, SCENE 2.   Afternoon

To open: General interior lighting

Cue 4	**Pauline:** "... blame you for."	(Page 49)
	Black-out	

ACT II, SCENE 2.   Evening

To open: Pendant, table lamp on

Cue 5	**Barry** takes **Janice**'s hand	(Page 57)
	Fade to black-out	

EFFECTS PLOT

ACT I

ACT II

MADE AND PRINTED IN GREAT BRITAIN BY
LATIMER TREND & COMPANY LTD, PLYMOUTH
MADE IN ENGLAND